This address book belongs to

NAME ....

ADDRESS ....

....

....

TEL ....

FAX ....

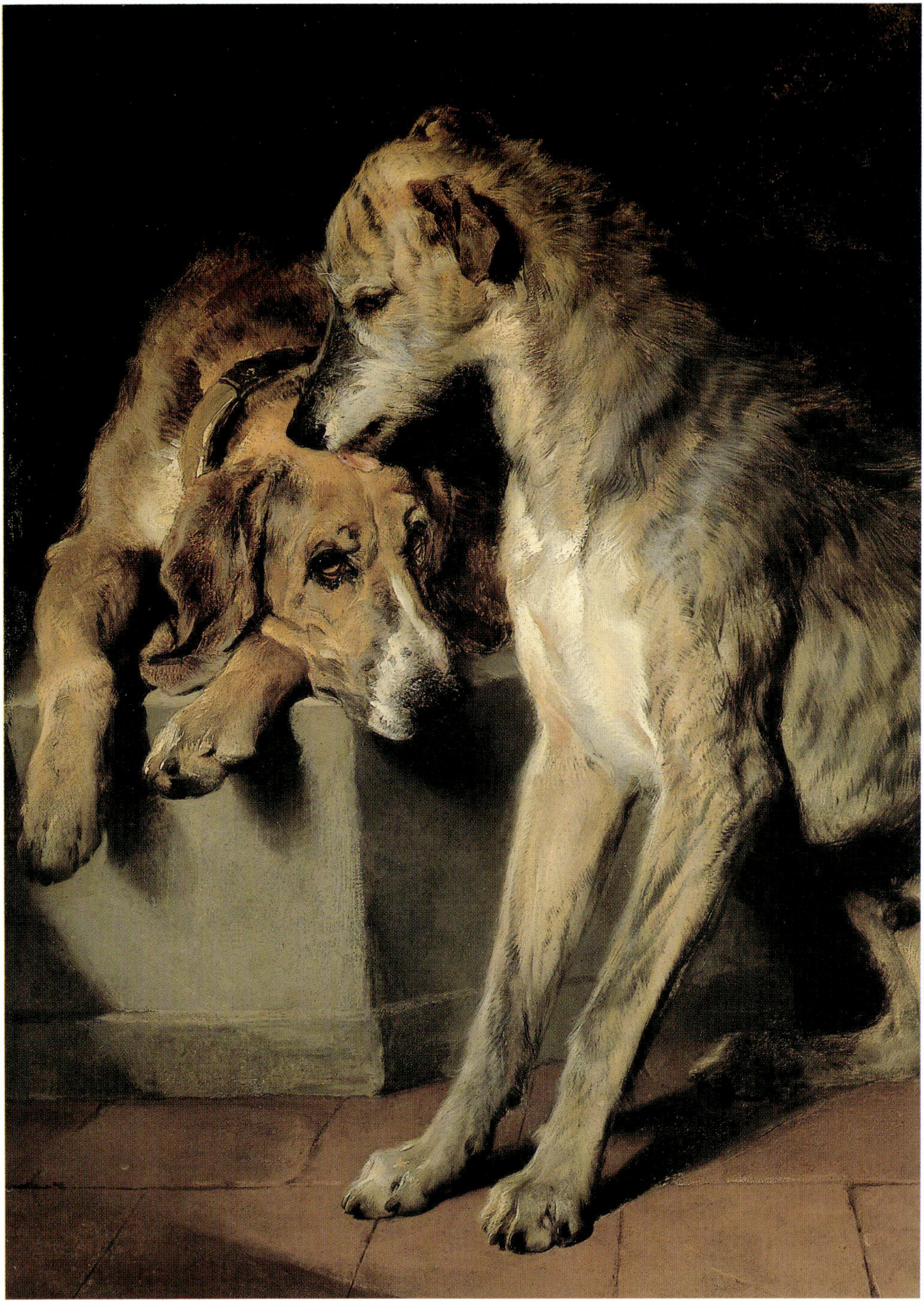

Address Book

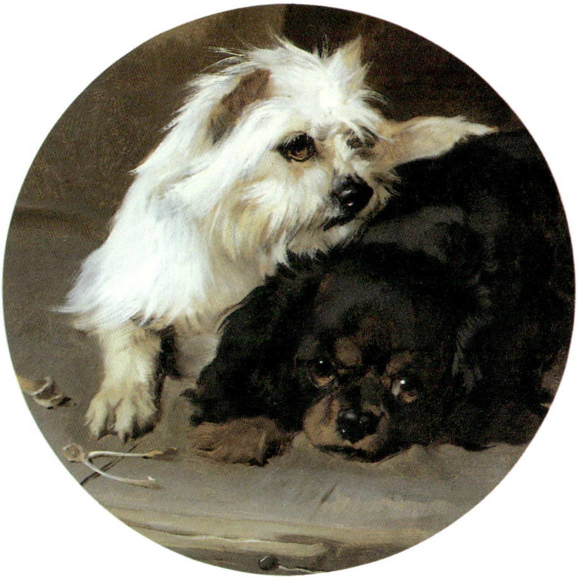

from

DOG PAINTING

1840~1940

A social history of the dog in art

WILLIAM SECORD

First published 1992, 1993, 1994, 1995, 1996

ISBN 1 85149 164 3

Published by the Antique Collectors' Club Ltd.

Illustration acknowledgements

Arthur Ackermann & Son, Ltd.; The American Kennel Club; Mrs. Vincent Astor; Bellechasse Antiques; Pat Beresford; Bonhams; Mario Buatta; The National Gallery of Canada, Ottawa; Christie's; Christie's South Kensington; The Dog Museum, St. Louis; Exclusively Dogs; Mr. and Mrs. Robert Franzblau; Richard Green; The Richard D. Hammond Collection; Iona Antiques; Mrs. Walter M. Jeffords; Mr. and Mrs. William Kendrick; MacConnal-Mason Fine Paintings; Mrs. Gwynne G. McDevitt; Mr. and Mrs. David Morris; The National Portrait Gallery; private collectors; Her Majesty the Queen; Mrs. Damon Raike; Roger Rechler; Mr. and Mrs. N.J. Reese; Mr. and Mrs. John H. Remer, Jnr.; Dr. and Mrs. Richard Rothman; Frances G. Scaife; Mr. and Mrs. Michael Svirsky; The Tate Gallery; The Tryon Gallery.

Frontispiece: Foxhound and Deerhound, 1839, Edwin Landseer

Printed in England
by the Antique Collectors' Club Ltd., Woodbridge, Suffolk, IP12 1DS
on Consort Royal Supreme Satin from Donside Mills, Aberdeen, Scotland

Foreword

Nineteenth century paintings of dogs have been of interest to pure-bred dog fanciers for decades. In the last ten years or so, however, they have come to the attention of a new and appreciative public.

Whether depicting a highly bred canine, a sporting dog in the field or a beloved pet, the appeal of dog paintings is obvious. They strike a responsive chord in all of us, for even if we need to reach back into the early years of our childhood, there are few of us indeed who have not been touched by the love of a dog.

Over the last few years I have noticed a significant change in collectors' attitudes towards dog paintings. What were once viewed as historical documents illustrating the history of a breed, are now being recognised as works of art.

The paintings in this address book are selected from the comprehensive volume, *Dog Painting, 1840-1940: A Social History of the Dog in Art,* and represent only a few of the wide variety of breeds and fine artists to be found among this increasingly popular genre.

William Secord
President
William Secord Gallery, Inc.
New York

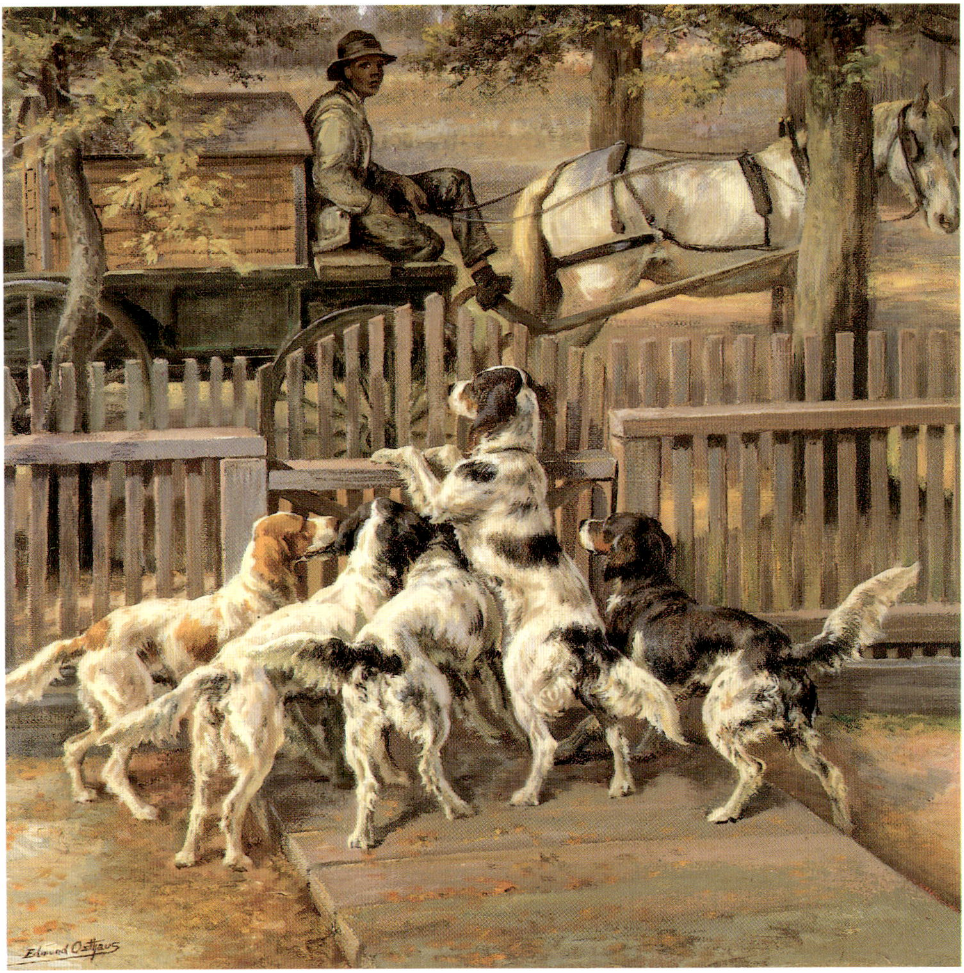

English Setters, c.1900, Edmund Osthaus.

The oak and metal dog kennel seen here was the typical transportation for dogs in the United States at the time this picture was painted, and remained so for many years.

About this book

An address book faithfully preserves the details of cherished friends as well as useful contacts, both sources of amusement and duty. It is thus comparable to that symbol of fidelity and trust throughout the ages: man's best friend, servant and dependable ally – the dog.

The publishers would like to thank Bill Secord for writing his wonderful book *Dog Painting* and for allowing them to use some of the illustrations in this address book.

Dogs are illustrated in many different moods and environments, enlivening the pages with the colourful character of dozens of breeds, each with its own attraction and purpose, whether for sport or for show, for domestic use or simply as an adored pet. Comparison of paintings of a particular breed also enable the changes in its development over the years to be traced.

These portraits give pleasure as well as relief to the steady record of names, places and numbers every human life accumulates.

It is hoped that for many years this book will give pleasure to people who love dogs.

A note on the illustrations

All the illustrations in this book have been taken from the Antique Collectors' Club publication *Dog Painting 1840-1940* by William Secord. In order to show as great a variety as possible of the 450 paintings illustrated in that book, we have in some cases shown only significant details here.

Wherever possible a date or circa date has been given to each illustration. However, in the case of artists who produced a great body of work, it is difficult to give realistic dates, unless, of course, paintings are dated, or an early/late style is indicated. A similar problem arises with artists about whose work and career little is known.

Important telephone numbers

DOCTOR:	BUILDER: ....
POLICE:	PLUMBER: ....
VETERINARY SURGEON:	CREDIT CARD LOSS: ....
ELECTRICITY:	DENTIST: ....
WATER:	TAXI: ....
TELEPHONE:	GARAGE: ....
BANK:	INSURANCE: ....
....	....
....	....
....	....
....	....
....	....
....	....
....	....
....	....
....	....

A

NAME

ADDRESS

TEL

FAX

NAME

ADDRESS

TEL

FAX

NAME

ADDRESS

TEL

FAX

NAME

ADDRESS

TEL

FAX

NAME

ADDRESS

TEL

FAX

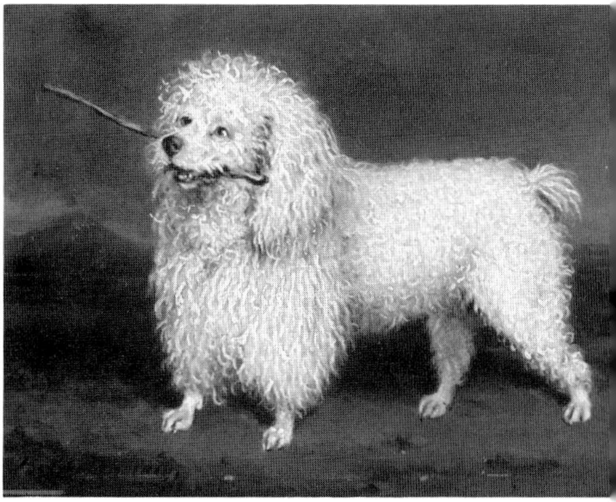

Maltese Terrier, 1819, Henry Bernard Chalon.

A

NAME

ADDRESS

TEL

FAX

NAME

ADDRESS

TEL

FAX

NAME

ADDRESS

TEL

FAX

NAME

ADDRESS

TEL

FAX

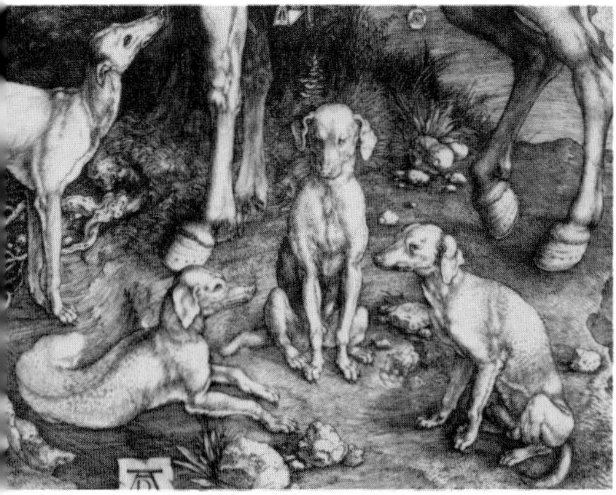

Greyhounds, 1501, Albrecht Dürer.

NAME

ADDRESS

TEL

FAX

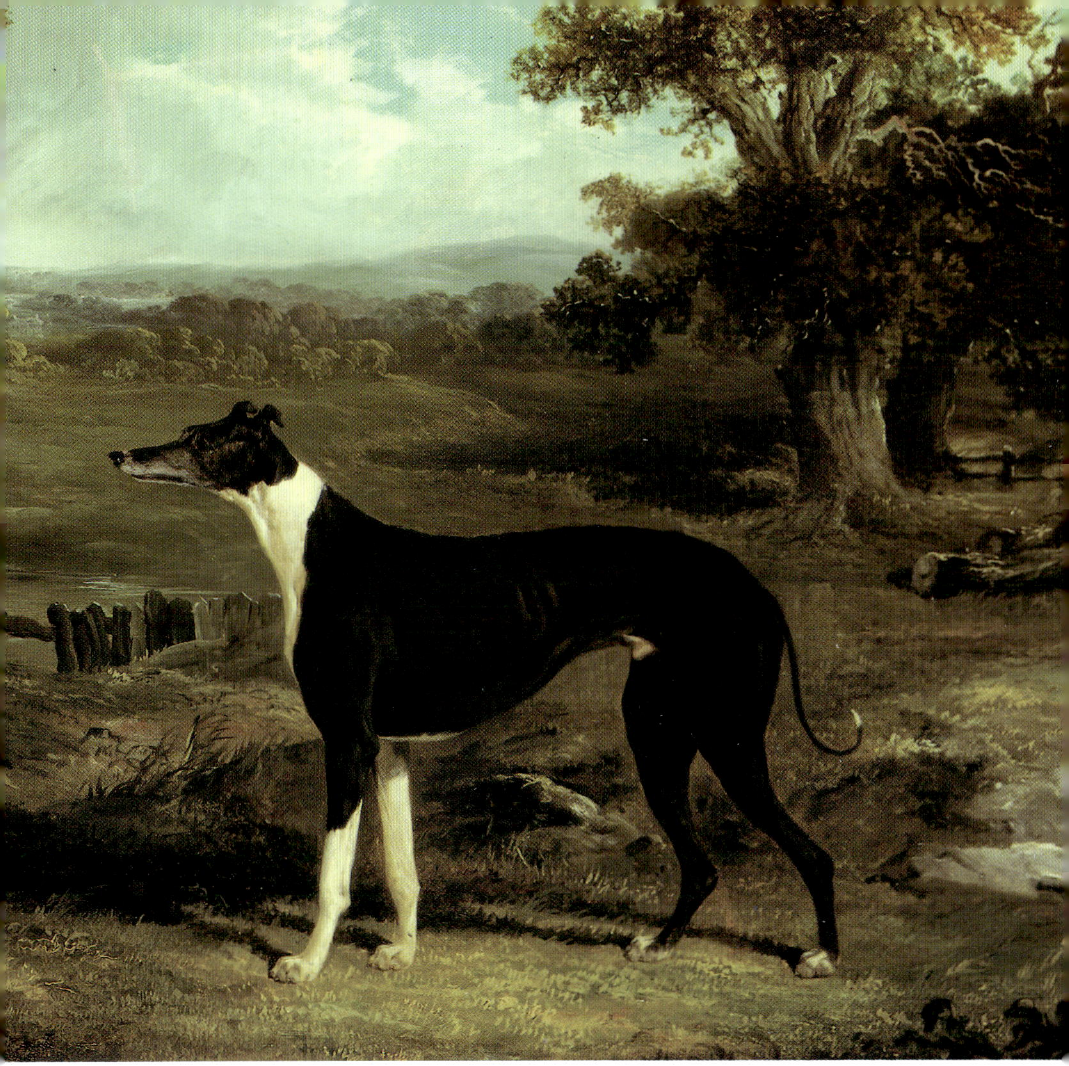

Greyhound, John Frederick Herring, Snr.

NAME ....

....

ADDRESS ....

....

....

....

TEL ....

....

FAX ....

NAME ....

....

ADDRESS ....

....

....

....

TEL ....

....

FAX ....

A

NAME

ADDRESS

TEL

FAX

NAME

ADDRESS

TEL

FAX

NAME

ADDRESS

TEL

FAX

NAME

ADDRESS

TEL

FAX

NAME

ADDRESS

TEL

FAX

NAME

ADDRESS

TEL

FAX

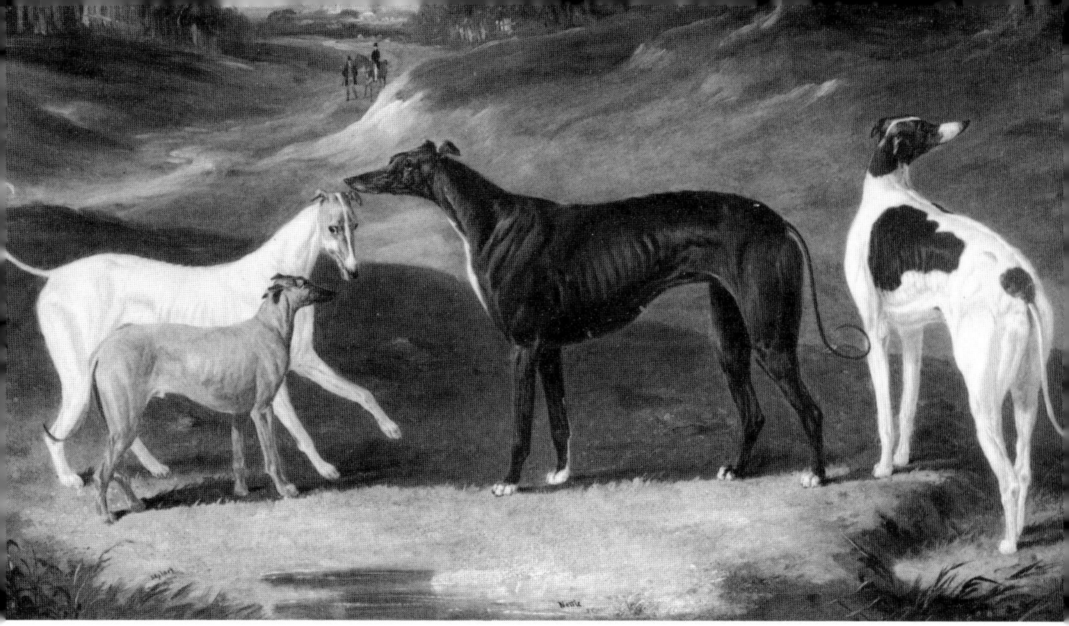

NAME ....

....

ADDRESS ....

....

....

....

TEL ....

....

FAX ....

NAME ....

....

ADDRESS ....

....

....

....

TEL ....

....

FAX ....

NAME ....

....

ADDRESS ....

....

....

....

TEL ....

....

FAX ....

NAME ....

....

ADDRESS ....

....

....

....

TEL ....

....

FAX ....

Greyhounds, 1829, John Frederick Herring, Snr.

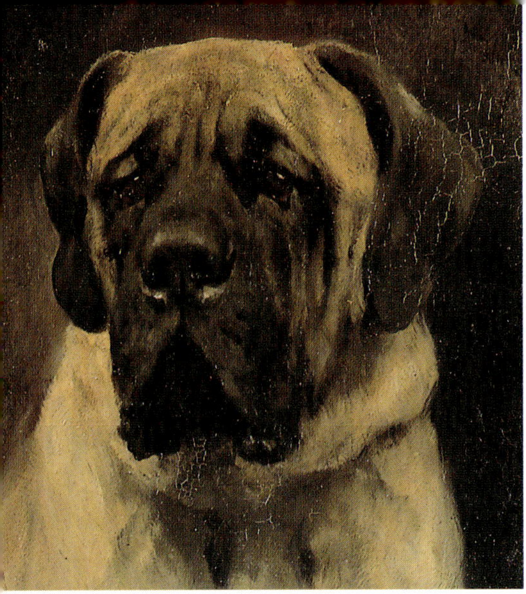

Mastiff, 1930, A. Wardle.

NAME ....

....

ADDRESS ....

....

....

....

TEL ....

....

FAX ....

NAME ....

....

ADDRESS ....

....

....

....

TEL ....

....

FAX ....

NAME ....

....

ADDRESS ....

....

....

....

TEL ....

....

FAX ....

NAME ....

....

ADDRESS ....

....

....

....

TEL ....

....

FAX ....

NAME ....

....

ADDRESS ....

....

....

....

TEL ....

....

FAX ....

A

What the lion is to the cat, the Mastiff is to the dog, the noblest of the family. Anon

NAME ....

....

ADDRESS ....

....

....

....

TEL ....

....

FAX ....

NAME ....

....

ADDRESS ....

....

....

....

TEL ....

....

FAX ....

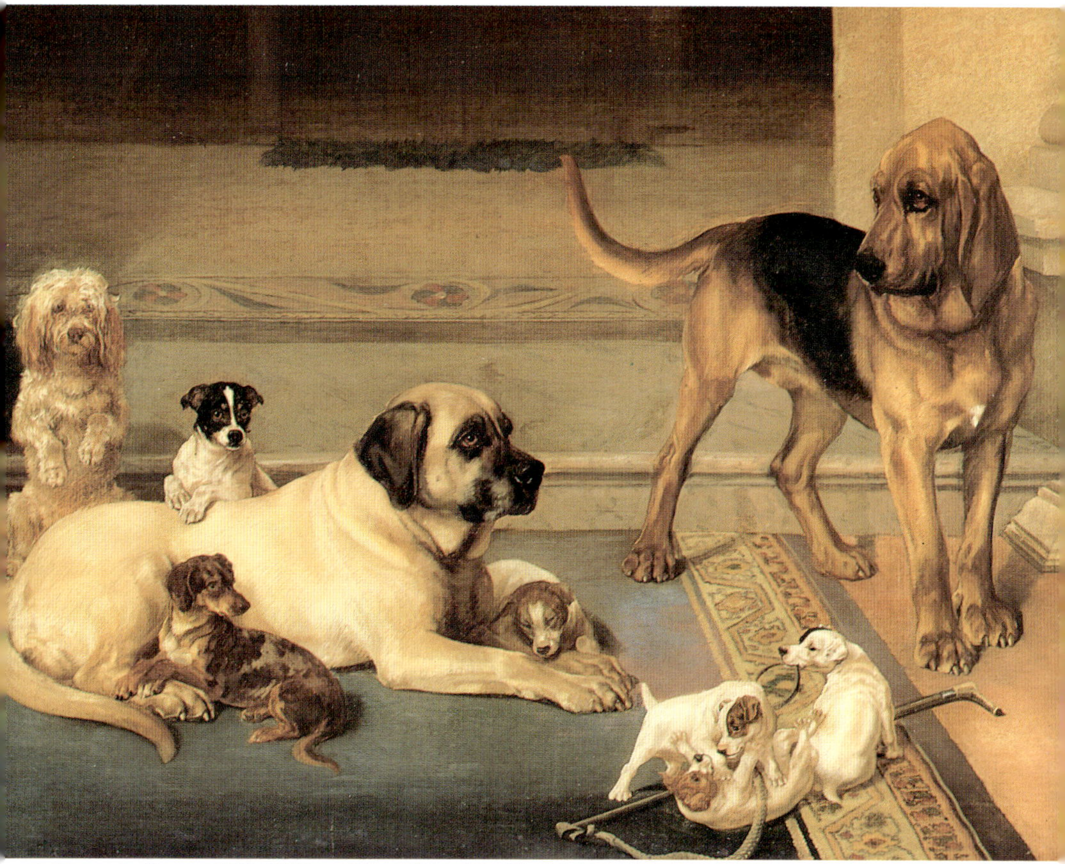

A Domestic Scene, 1888, William Henry Hamilton Trood.

B

NAME

ADDRESS

TEL

FAX

NAME

ADDRESS

TEL

FAX

NAME

ADDRESS

TEL

FAX

NAME

ADDRESS

TEL

FAX

NAME

ADDRESS

TEL

FAX

NAME

ADDRESS

TEL

FAX

I am his Highness' dog at Kew,
Pray tell me sir, whose dog are you?
Anon.

B

NAME ....
....
ADDRESS ....
....
....
....
TEL ....
....
FAX ....

NAME ....
....
ADDRESS ....
....
....
....
TEL ....
....
FAX ....

NAME ....
....
ADDRESS ....
....
....
....
TEL ....
....
FAX ....

NAME ....
....
ADDRESS ....
....
....
....
TEL ....
....
FAX ....

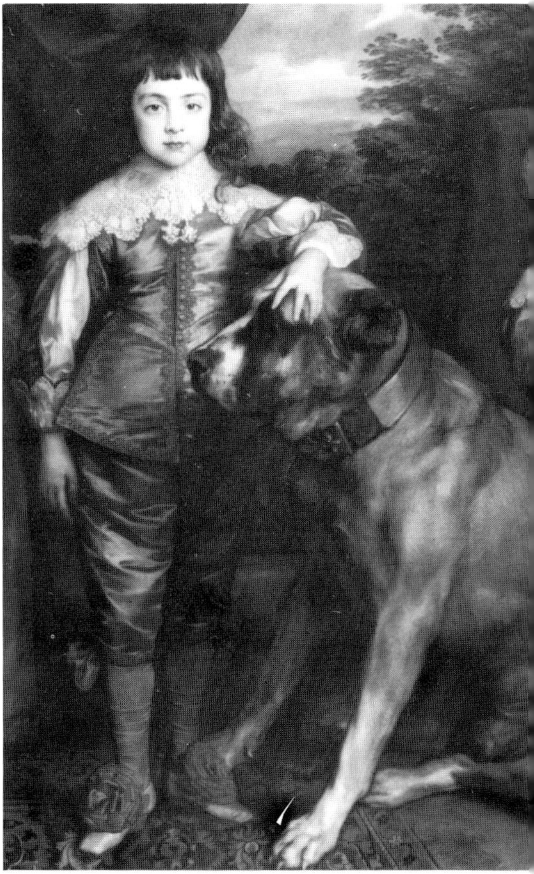

Mastiff, c.1630, Anthony Van Dyck.

B

NAME

ADDRESS

TEL

FAX

NAME

ADDRESS

TEL

FAX

NAME

ADDRESS

TEL

FAX

NAME

ADDRESS

TEL

FAX

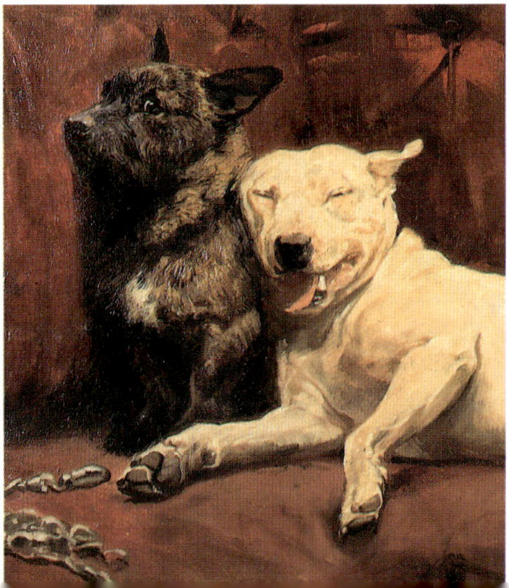

NAME

ADDRESS

TEL

FAX

Bull Terrier and Scottish Terrier, 1892,
M.C.W. Flower.

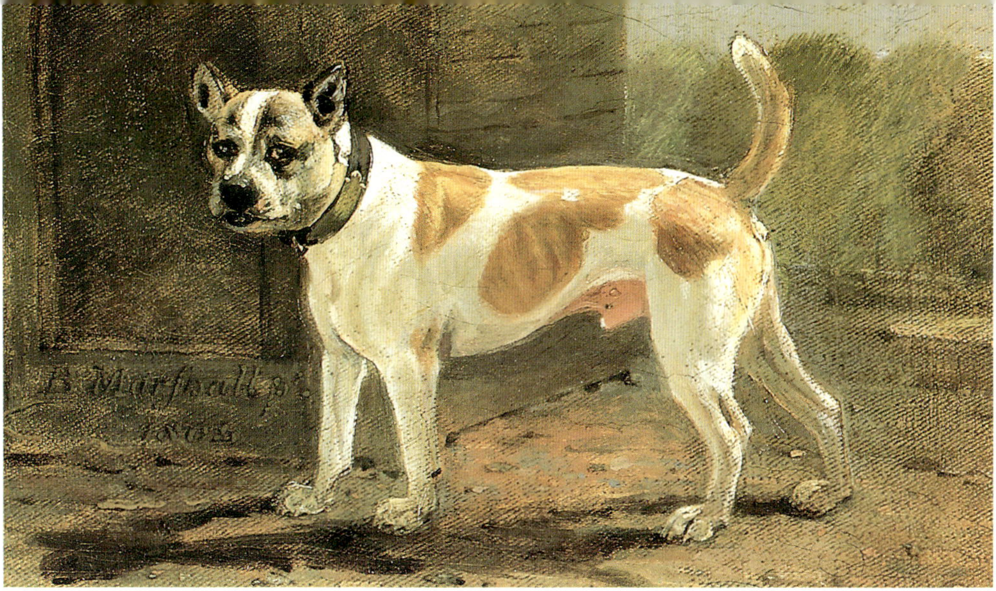

Bulldog/Terrier cross, 1804, B. Marshall.

NAME ....

....

ADDRESS ....

....

....

....

TEL ....

....

FAX ....

NAME ....

....

ADDRESS ....

....

....

....

TEL ....

....

FAX ....

NAME ....

....

ADDRESS ....

....

....

....

TEL ....

....

FAX ....

NAME ....

....

ADDRESS ....

....

....

....

TEL ....

....

FAX ....

B

NAME

ADDRESS

TEL

FAX

NAME

ADDRESS

TEL

FAX

NAME

ADDRESS

TEL

FAX

NAME

ADDRESS

TEL

FAX

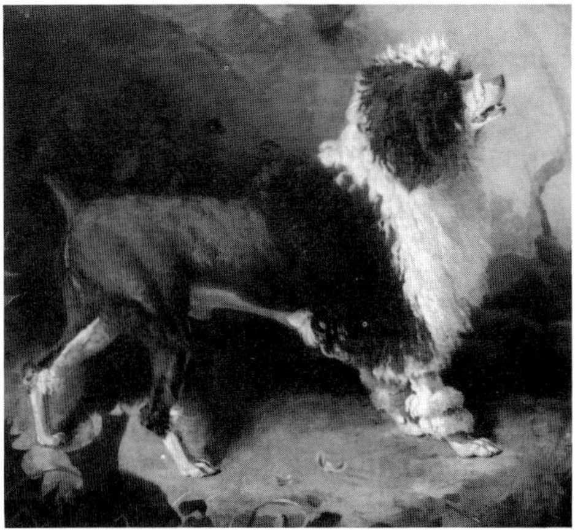

NAME

ADDRESS

TEL

FAX

Poodle, 1793, Richard Ramsey Reinagle.

B

NAME

ADDRESS

TEL

FAX

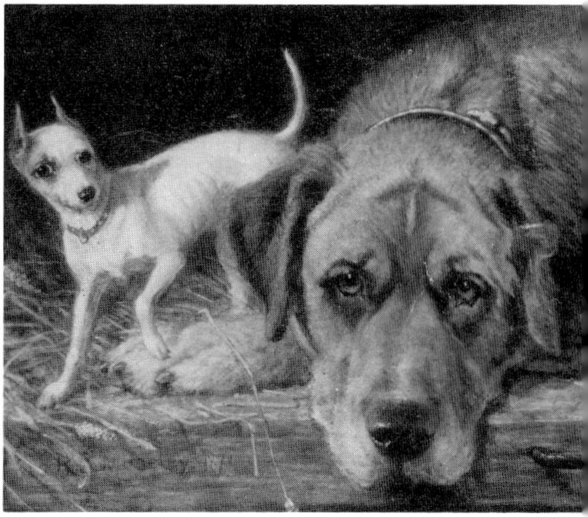

NAME

ADDRESS

TEL

FAX

NAME

ADDRESS

TEL

FAX

NAME

ADDRESS

TEL

FAX

NAME

ADDRESS

TEL

FAX

Mastiff with Terrier, 1871, R.S. Moseley.

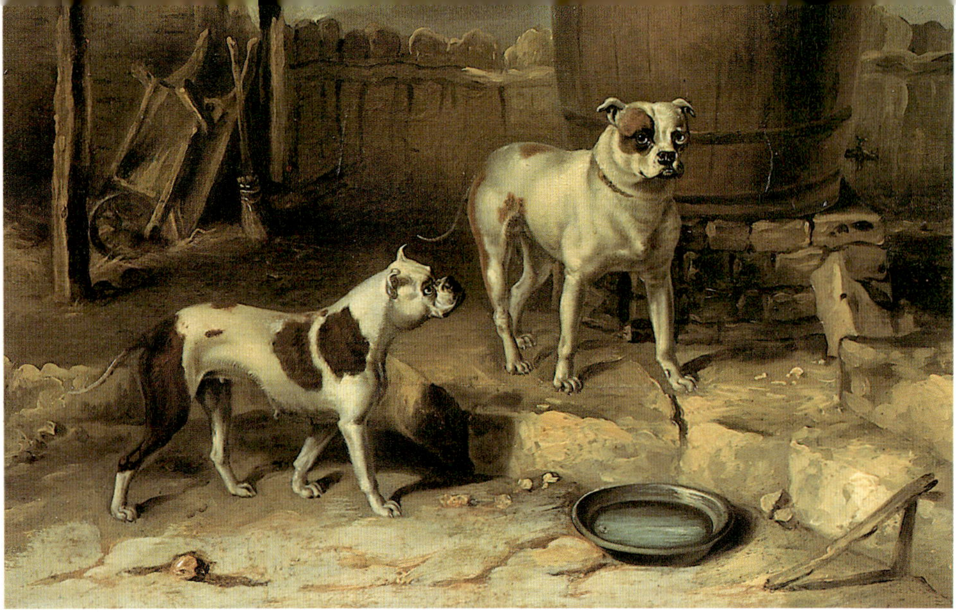

Bulldogs, 1817, Abraham Cooper.

NAME ....

....

ADDRESS ....

....

....

....

TEL ....

....

FAX ....

NAME ....

....

ADDRESS ....

....

....

....

TEL ....

....

FAX ....

NAME ....

....

ADDRESS ....

....

....

....

TEL ....

....

FAX ....

NAME ....

....

ADDRESS ....

....

....

....

TEL ....

....

FAX ....

C

NAME ....

....

ADDRESS ....

....

....

....

TEL ....

....

FAX ....

NAME ....

....

ADDRESS ....

....

....

....

TEL ....

....

FAX ....

NAME ....

....

ADDRESS ....

....

....

....

TEL ....

....

FAX ....

NAME ....

....

ADDRESS ....

....

....

....

TEL ....

....

FAX ....

NAME ....

....

ADDRESS ....

....

....

....

TEL ....

....

FAX ....

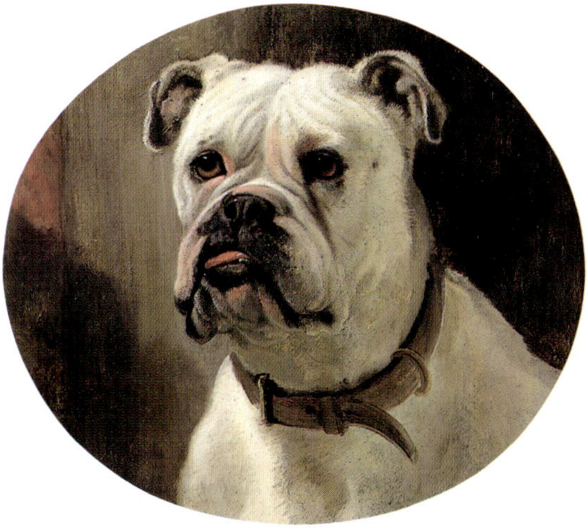

Bulldog, c.1870, George Earl.

C

NAME

ADDRESS

TEL

FAX

NAME

ADDRESS

TEL

FAX

NAME

ADDRESS

TEL

FAX

NAME

ADDRESS

TEL

FAX

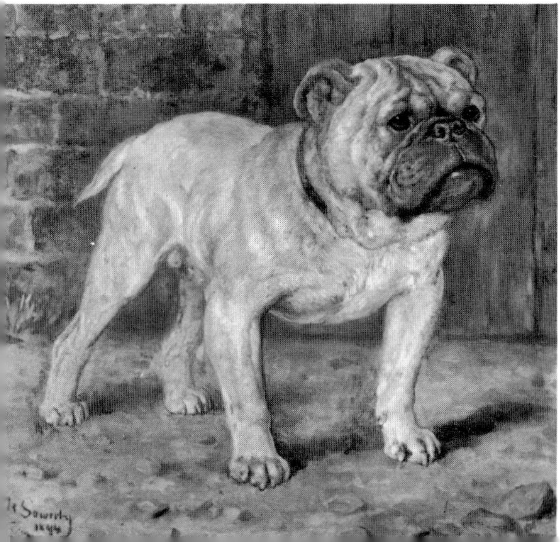

NAME

ADDRESS

TEL

FAX

Bulldog, 1894, Kole Sowerby.

C

NAME

ADDRESS

TEL

FAX

NAME

ADDRESS

TEL

FAX

NAME

ADDRESS

TEL

FAX

NAME

ADDRESS

TEL

FAX

NAME

ADDRESS

TEL

FAX

NAME

ADDRESS

TEL

FAX

C

'They say he's a friendly dog . . . as clever as a Christian, always in a good temper, always friendly, always well-behaved. You don't often see an animal so gentlemanly at that age.'
Marcel Proust

NAME

ADDRESS

TEL

FAX

NAME

ADDRESS

TEL

FAX

NAME

ADDRESS

TEL

FAX

NAME

ADDRESS

TEL

FAX

NAME

ADDRESS

TEL

FAX

NAME

ADDRESS

TEL

FAX

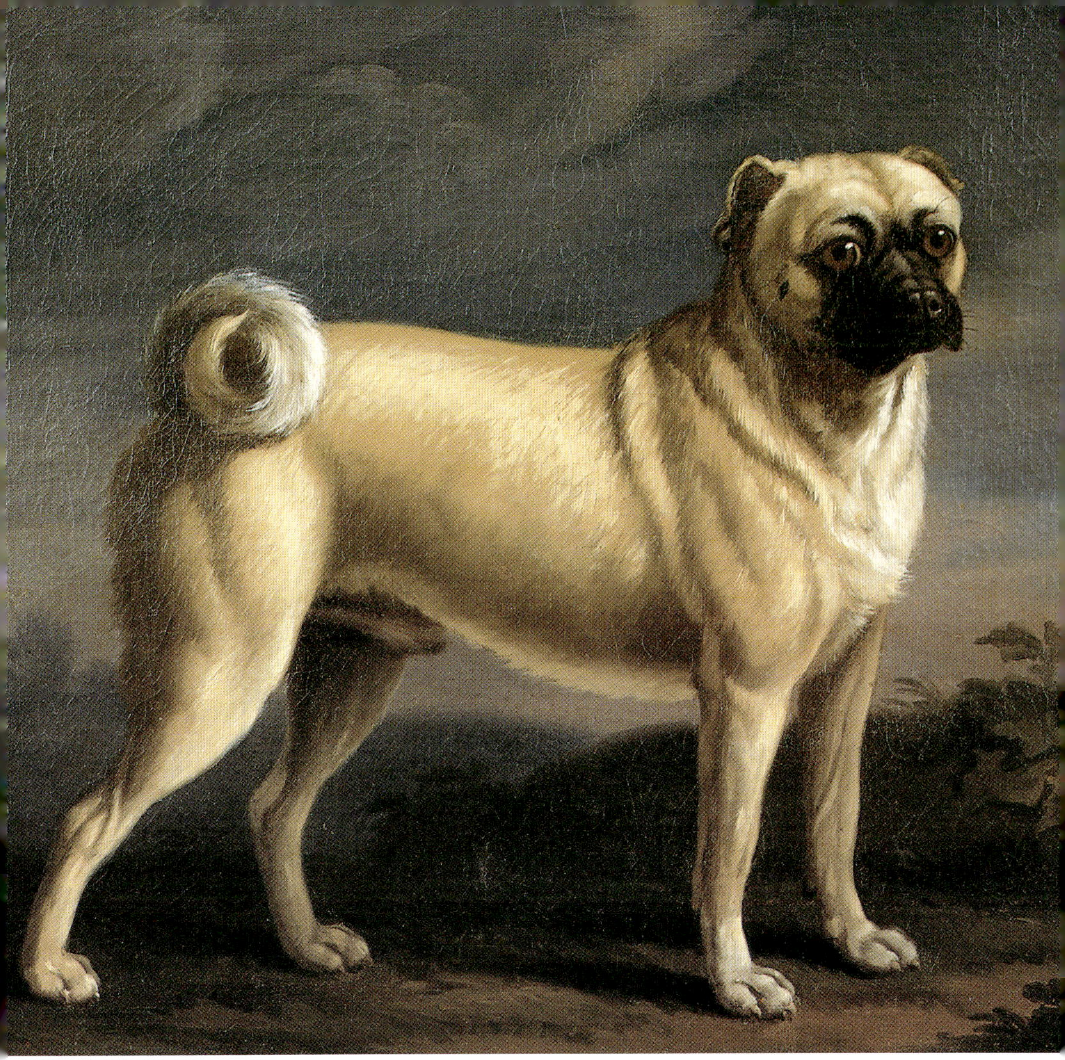

Pug, early 19th century, Richard Ramsey Reinagle.

NAME ....

....

ADDRESS ....

....

....

....

TEL ....

....

FAX ....

NAME ....

....

ADDRESS ....

....

....

....

TEL ....

....

FAX ....

C

NAME

ADDRESS

TEL

FAX

NAME

ADDRESS

TEL

FAX

NAME

ADDRESS

TEL

FAX

NAME

ADDRESS

TEL

FAX

NAME

ADDRESS

TEL

FAX

NAME

ADDRESS

TEL

FAX

C

NAME

ADDRESS

TEL

FAX

NAME

ADDRESS

TEL

FAX

NAME

ADDRESS

TEL

FAX

NAME

ADDRESS

TEL

FAX

NAME

ADDRESS

TEL

FAX

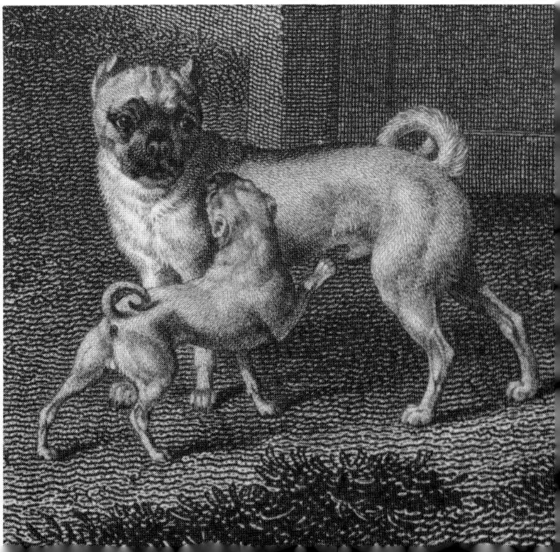

Pugs, 1803, Philip Reinagle.

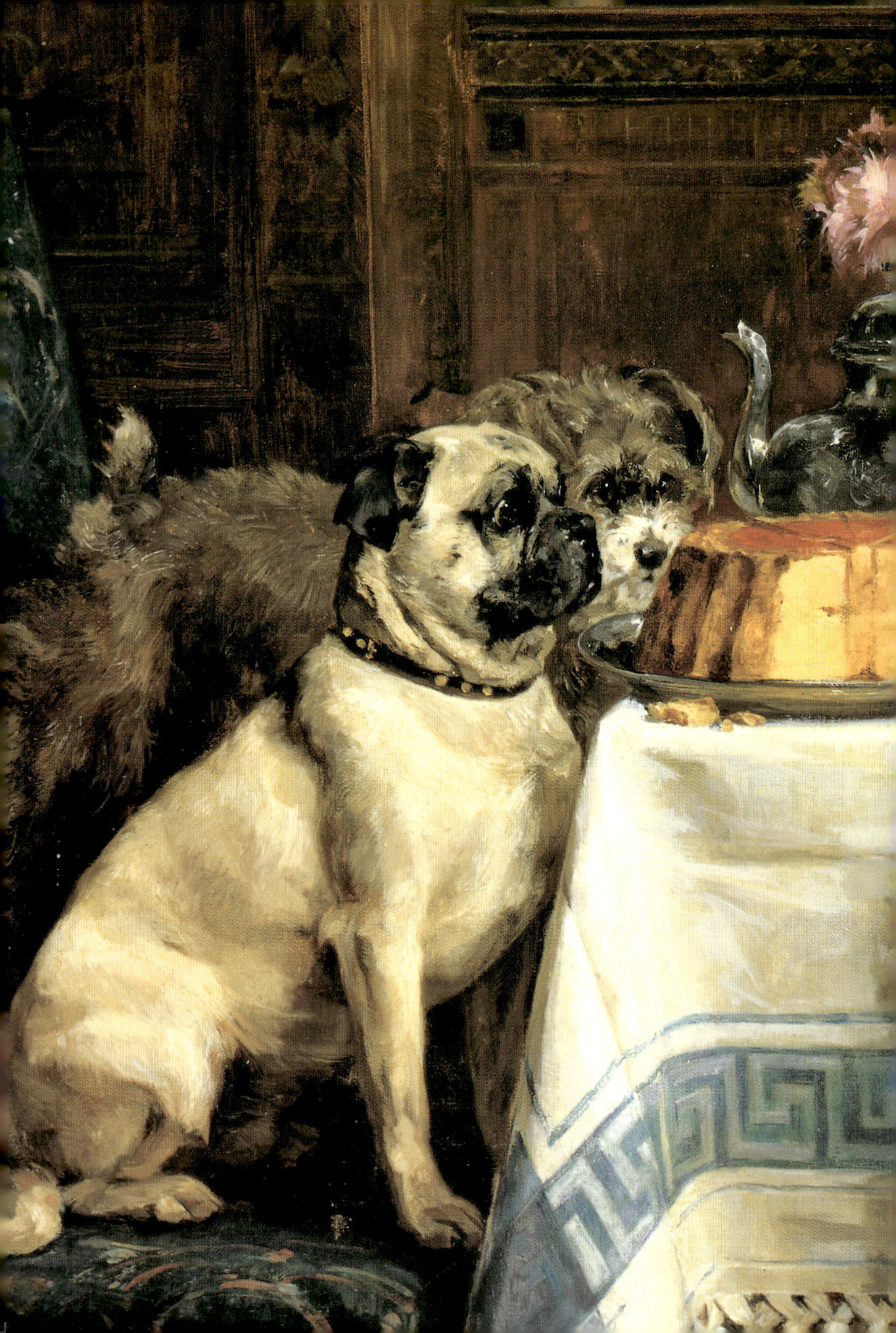

D

God created man; then seeing how weak he was, gave him the dog. Toussenel

NAME

ADDRESS

TEL

FAX

NAME

ADDRESS

TEL

FAX

NAME

ADDRESS

TEL

FAX

NAME

ADDRESS

TEL

FAX

NAME

ADDRESS

TEL

FAX

Pug and Terrier, 1891, Charles van den Eycken.

Pug, 1875, Walter Harrowing.

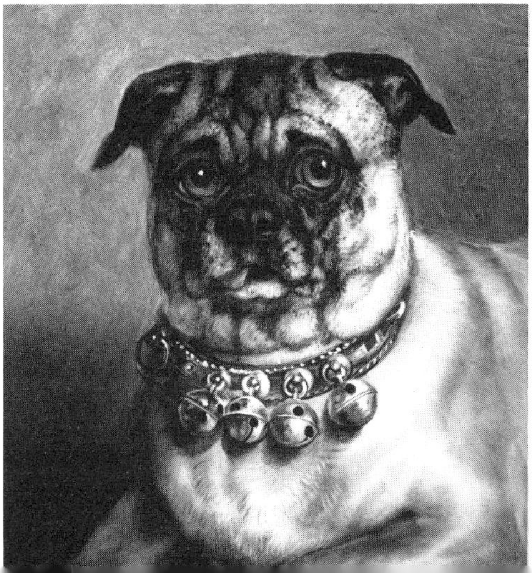

D

NAME

ADDRESS

TEL

FAX

NAME

ADDRESS

TEL

FAX

NAME

ADDRESS

TEL

FAX

NAME

ADDRESS

TEL

FAX

NAME

ADDRESS

TEL

FAX

NAME

ADDRESS

TEL

FAX

What kind of a life a dog . . . acquires, I have sometimes tried to imagine by kneeling or lying full length on the ground and looking up. The world then becomes strangely incomplete: one sees little but legs. E.V. Lucas

D

NAME

ADDRESS

TEL

FAX

NAME

ADDRESS

TEL

FAX

NAME

ADDRESS

TEL

FAX

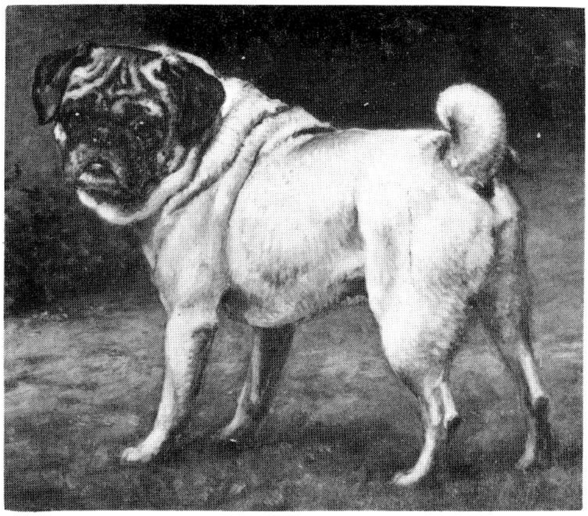
Pug, c.1895, Maud Earl.

NAME

ADDRESS

TEL

FAX

NAME

ADDRESS

TEL

FAX

D

Man is an animal that makes bargains; no other animal does this — one dog does not change a bone with another.
Adam Smith

NAME ....
....
ADDRESS ....
....
....
....
TEL ....
....
FAX ....

NAME ....
....
ADDRESS ....
....
....
....
TEL ....
....
FAX ....

NAME ....
....
ADDRESS ....
....
....
....
TEL ....
....
FAX ....

NAME ....
....
ADDRESS ....
....
....
....
TEL ....
....
FAX ....

NAME ....
....
ADDRESS ....
....
....
....
TEL ....
....
FAX ....

NAME ....
....
ADDRESS ....
....
....
....
TEL ....
....
FAX ....

Pug and Dachshund, 1875, John Sargent Noble.

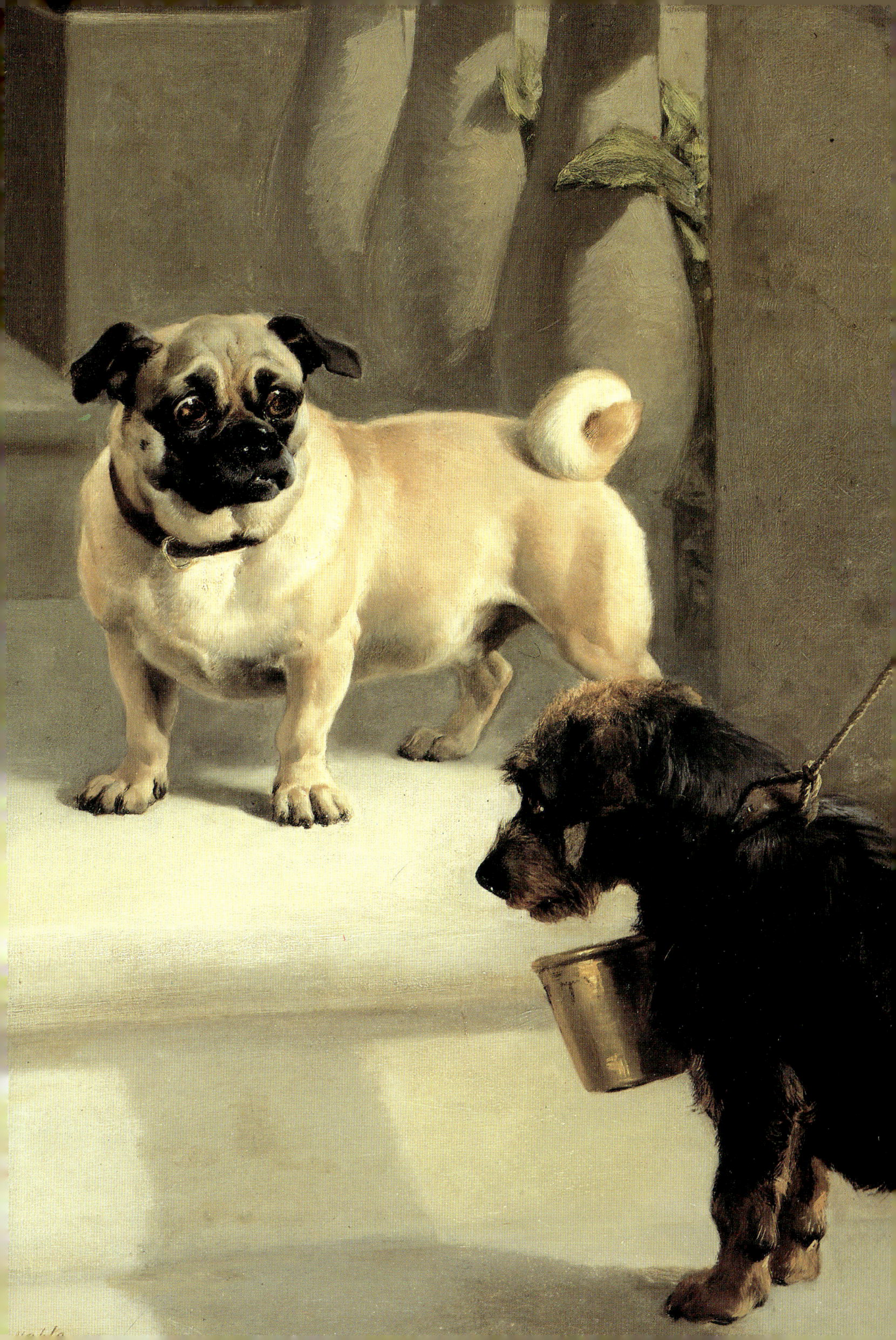

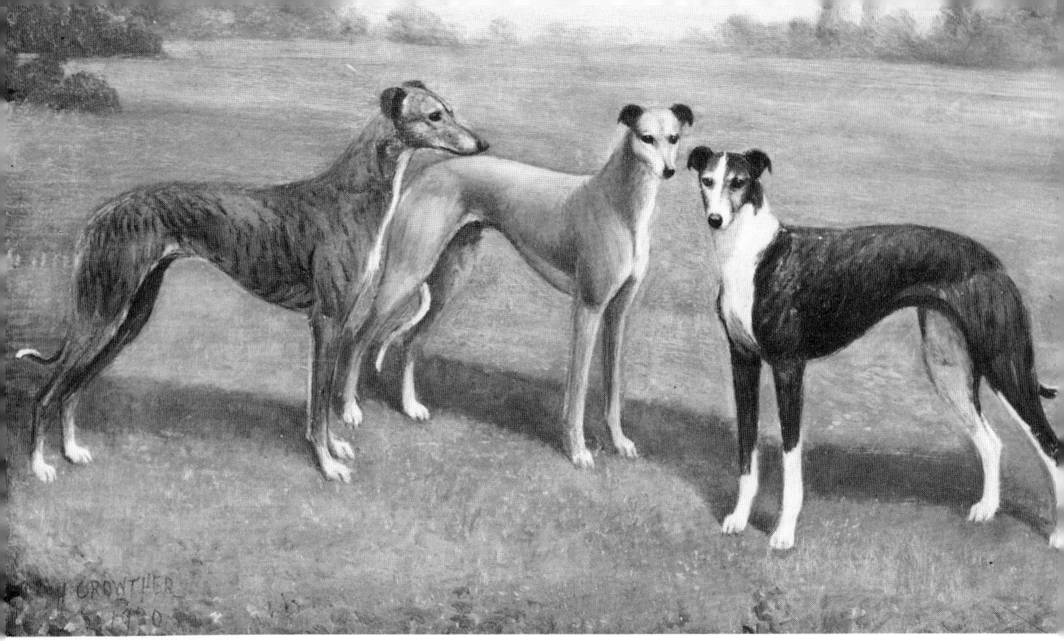

NAME

ADDRESS

TEL

FAX

NAME

ADDRESS

TEL

FAX

NAME

ADDRESS

TEL

FAX

NAME

ADDRESS

TEL

FAX

Greyhounds, 1930, Henry Crowther.

E

The more I see of men, the better I like my dog.
Frederick The Great

NAME

ADDRESS

TEL

FAX

NAME

ADDRESS

TEL

FAX

NAME

ADDRESS

TEL

FAX

NAME

ADDRESS

TEL

FAX

NAME

ADDRESS

TEL

FAX

NAME

ADDRESS

TEL

FAX

E

Brothers and sisters, I bid you beware
Of giving your heart to a dog to tear.
Rudyard Kipling

NAME

ADDRESS

TEL

FAX

NAME

ADDRESS

TEL

FAX

NAME

ADDRESS

TEL

FAX

NAME

ADDRESS

TEL

FAX

NAME

ADDRESS

TEL

FAX

NAME

ADDRESS

TEL

FAX

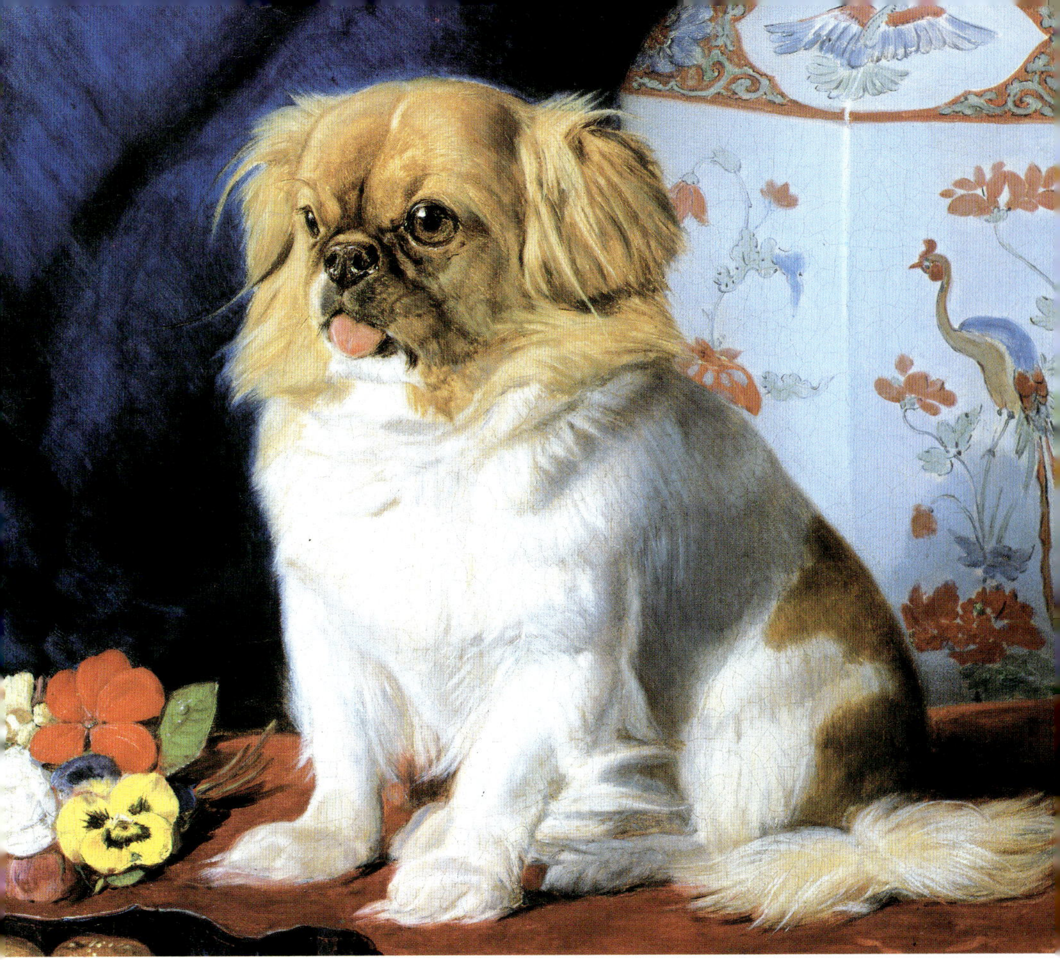
Pekingese, 1861, Friedrich Wilhelm Keyl.

NAME ....

....

ADDRESS ....

....

....

....

TEL ....

....

FAX ....

NAME ....

....

ADDRESS ....

....

....

....

TEL ....

....

FAX ....

E

NAME

ADDRESS

TEL

FAX

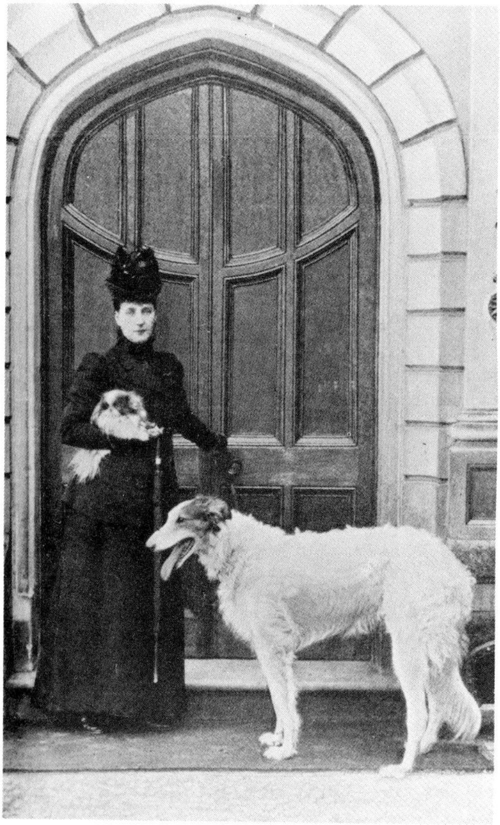

Princess Alexandra with her Pekingese and Borzoi, c.1895.

NAME

ADDRESS

TEL

FAX

NAME

ADDRESS

TEL

FAX

NAME

ADDRESS

TEL

FAX

E

NAME

ADDRESS

TEL

FAX

NAME

ADDRESS

TEL

FAX

NAME

ADDRESS

TEL

FAX

NAME

ADDRESS

TEL

FAX

NAME

ADDRESS

TEL

FAX

NAME

ADDRESS

TEL

FAX

F

NAME

ADDRESS

TEL

FAX

NAME

ADDRESS

TEL

FAX

NAME

ADDRESS

TEL

FAX

NAME

ADDRESS

TEL

FAX

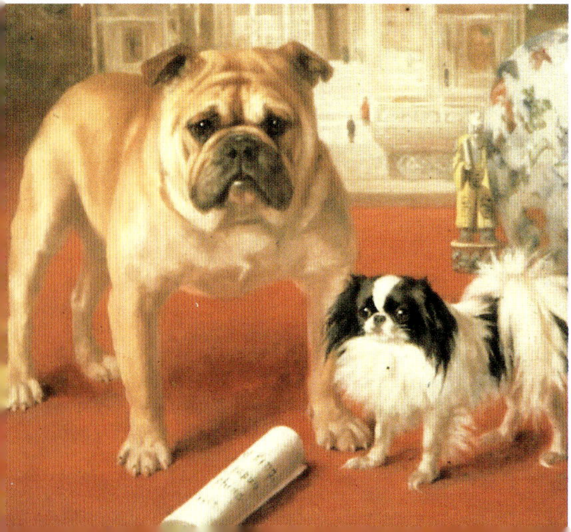

NAME

ADDRESS

TEL

FAX

Bulldog and Japanese Chin, 1902, F.L. Fairman.

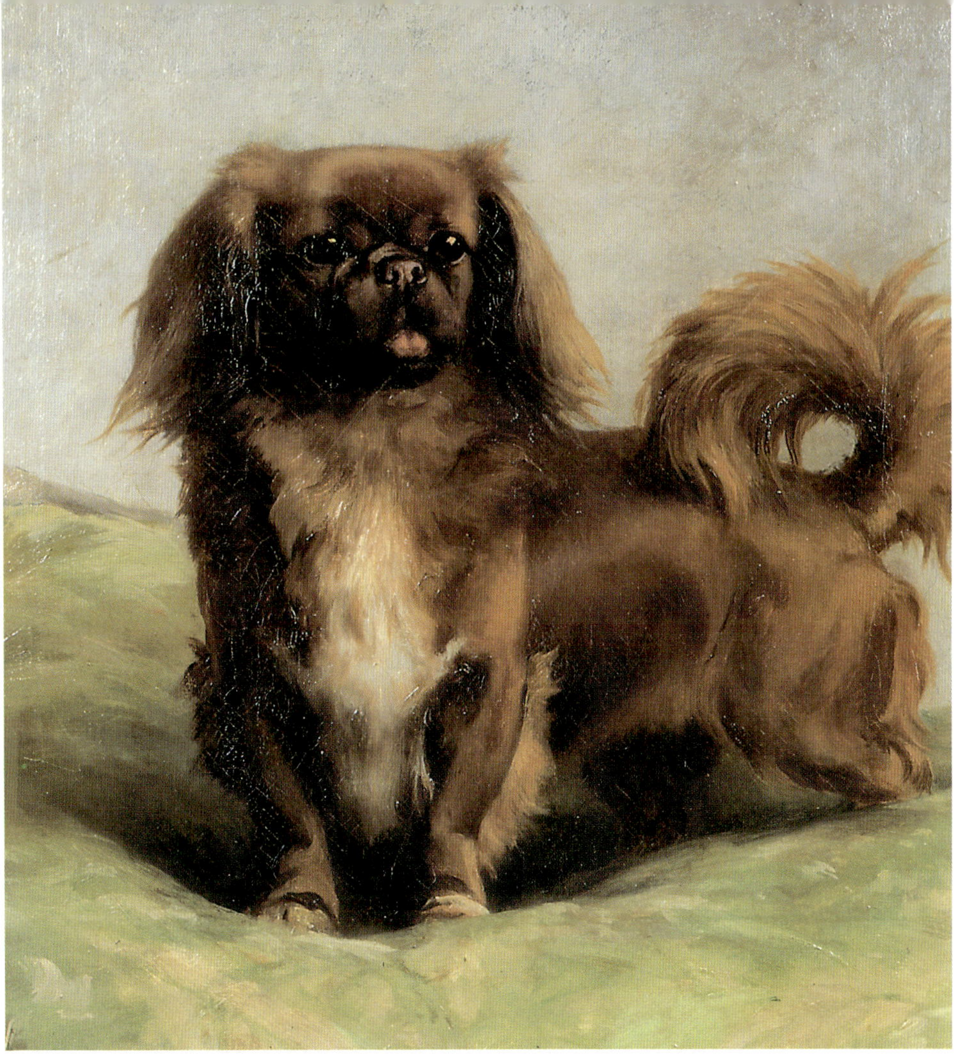

Pekingese, 1910, Percival Rosseau.

NAME ....

....

ADDRESS ....

....

....

....

TEL ....

....

FAX ....

NAME ....

....

ADDRESS ....

....

....

....

TEL ....

....

FAX ....

F

If you would invest in friendship, purchase a dog.
Le Baron Cooke

NAME

ADDRESS

TEL

FAX

NAME

ADDRESS

TEL

FAX

NAME

ADDRESS

TEL

FAX

NAME

ADDRESS

TEL

FAX

NAME

ADDRESS

TEL

FAX

NAME

ADDRESS

TEL

FAX

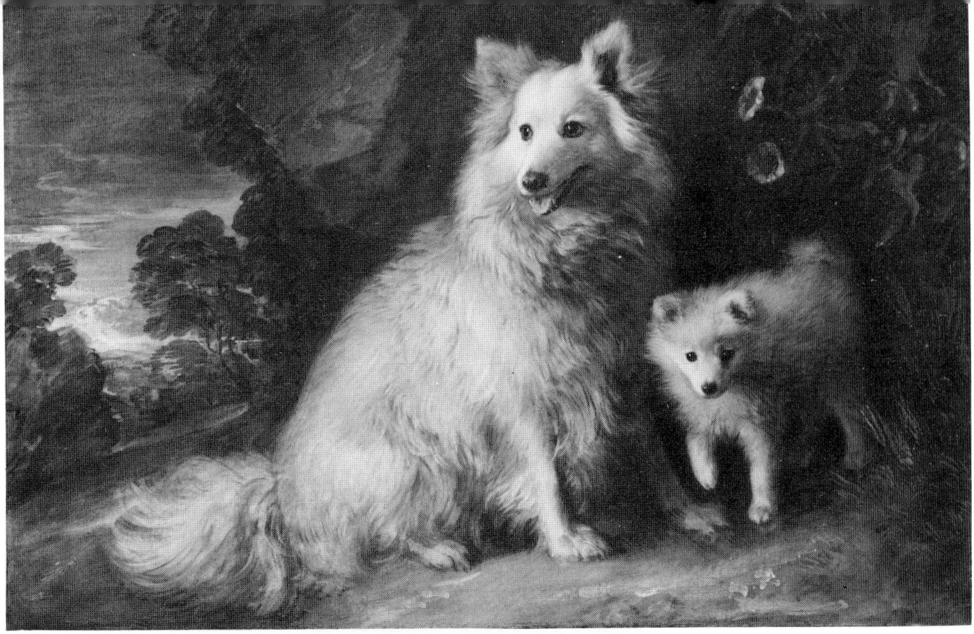

NAME ....

....

ADDRESS ....

....

....

....

TEL ....

....

FAX ....

NAME ....

....

ADDRESS ....

....

....

....

TEL ....

....

FAX ....

NAME ....

....

ADDRESS ....

....

....

....

TEL ....

....

FAX ....

NAME ....

....

ADDRESS ....

....

....

....

TEL ....

....

FAX ....

Pomeranian and puppy, c.1777, Thomas Gainsborough.

F

NAME

ADDRESS

TEL

FAX

NAME

ADDRESS

TEL

FAX

NAME

ADDRESS

TEL

FAX

NAME

ADDRESS

TEL

FAX

NAME

ADDRESS

TEL

FAX

NAME

ADDRESS

TEL

FAX

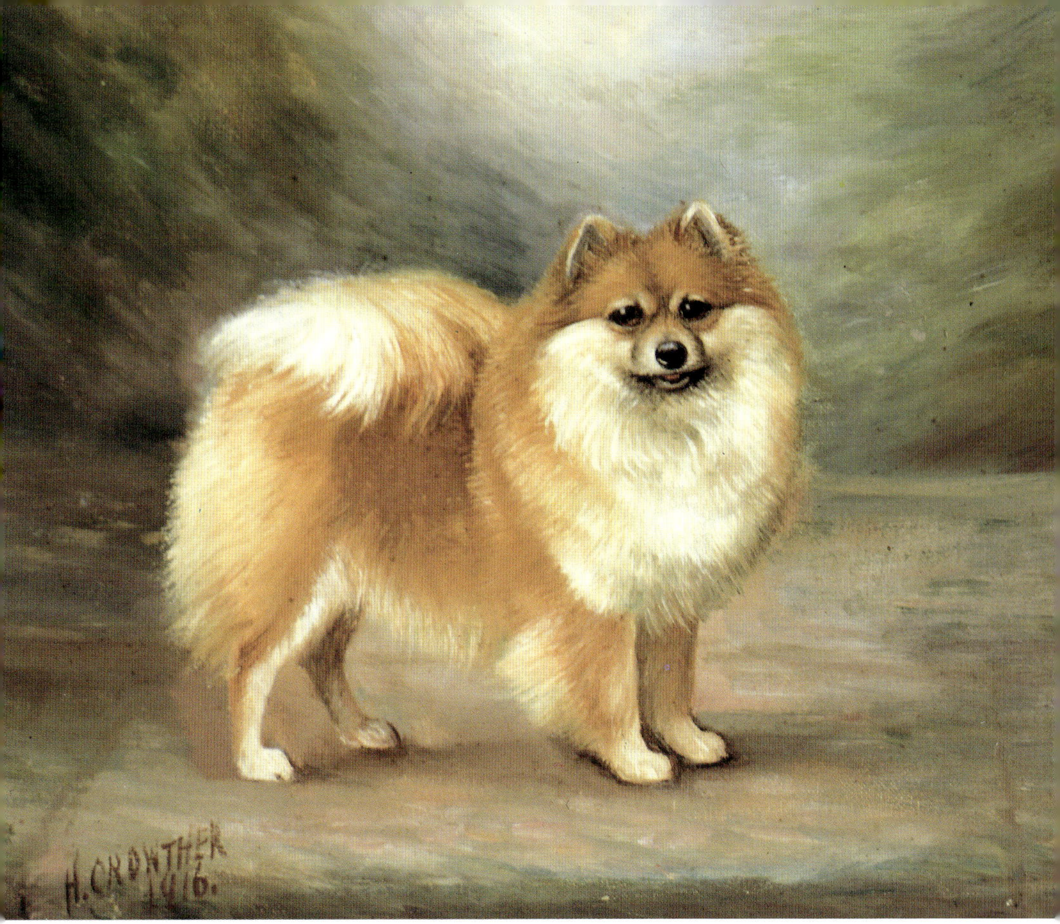

Pomeranian, 1916, Henry Crowther.

NAME ....

....

ADDRESS ....

....

....

....

TEL ....

....

FAX ....

NAME ....

....

ADDRESS ....

....

....

....

TEL ....

....

FAX ....

G

NAME

ADDRESS

TEL

FAX

NAME

ADDRESS

TEL

FAX

NAME

ADDRESS

TEL

FAX

NAME

ADDRESS

TEL

FAX

NAME

ADDRESS

TEL

FAX

NAME

ADDRESS

TEL

FAX

G

NAME

ADDRESS

TEL

FAX

NAME

ADDRESS

TEL

FAX

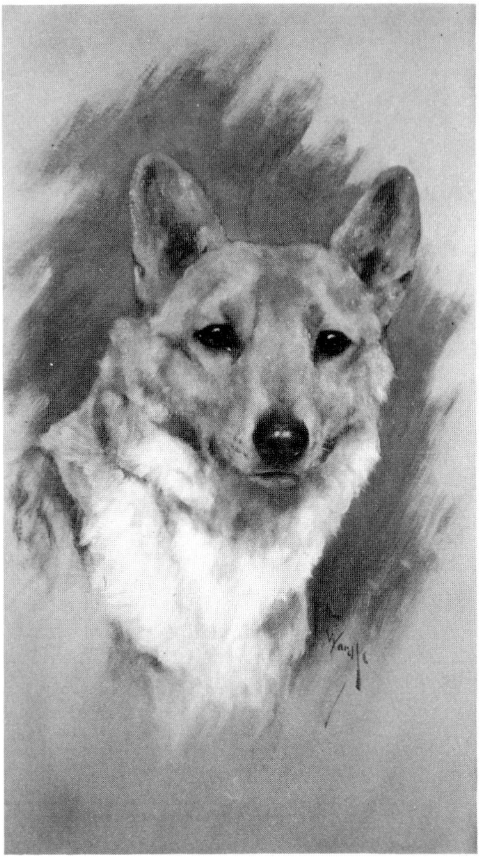

Corgi, c.1930, Arthur Wardle.

NAME

ADDRESS

TEL

FAX

NAME

ADDRESS

TEL

FAX

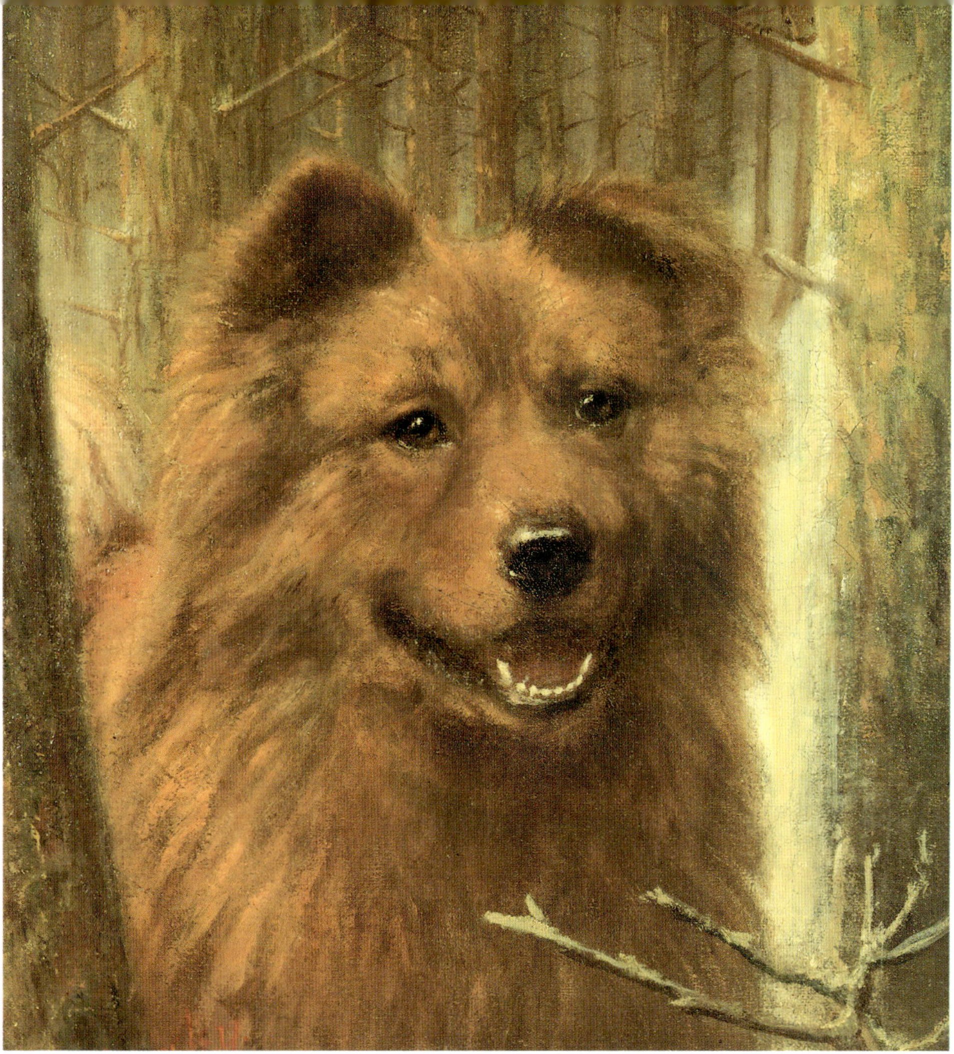

Chow-Chow, 1897, R.S. Moseley.

NAME ....

....

ADDRESS ....

....

....

....

TEL ....

....

FAX ....

NAME ....

....

ADDRESS ....

....

....

....

TEL ....

....

FAX ....

G

NAME

ADDRESS

TEL

FAX

NAME

ADDRESS

TEL

FAX

NAME

ADDRESS

TEL

FAX

NAME

ADDRESS

TEL

FAX

NAME

ADDRESS

TEL

FAX

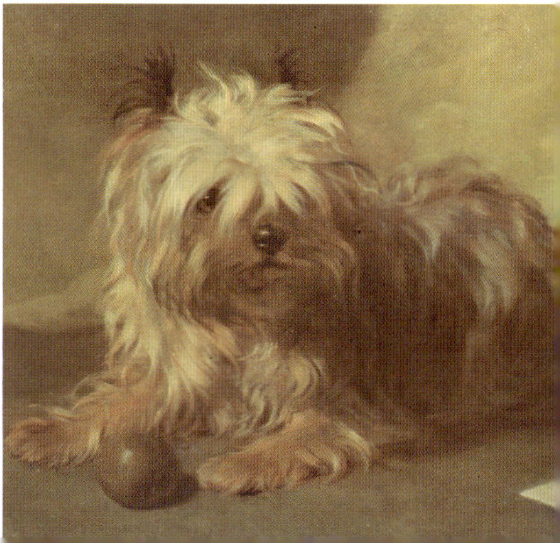

Yorkshire Terrier, 1877, English School.

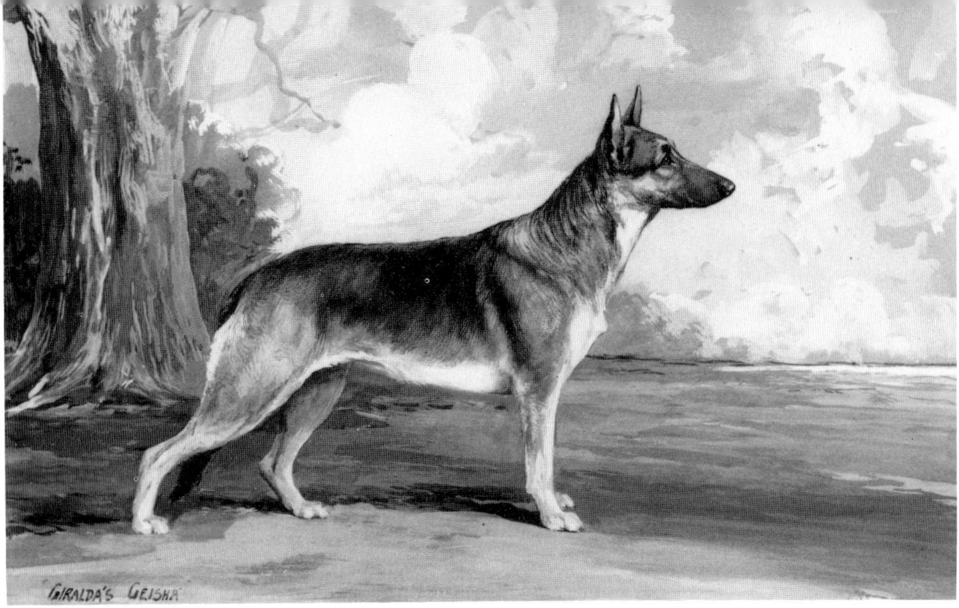

German Shepherd, 1936, Reuben Ward Binks.

NAME

ADDRESS

TEL

FAX

NAME

ADDRESS

TEL

FAX

NAME

ADDRESS

TEL

FAX

NAME

ADDRESS

TEL

FAX

G

What he most intensely dreams of is being taken out on walks, and the more you are able to indulge him the more he will adore you. Henry James

NAME

ADDRESS

TEL

FAX

NAME

ADDRESS

TEL

FAX

NAME

ADDRESS

TEL

FAX

NAME

ADDRESS

TEL

FAX

NAME

ADDRESS

TEL

FAX

NAME

ADDRESS

TEL

FAX

H

NAME

ADDRESS

TEL

FAX

NAME

ADDRESS

TEL

FAX

NAME

ADDRESS

TEL

FAX

NAME

ADDRESS

TEL

FAX

NAME

ADDRESS

TEL

FAX

NAME

ADDRESS

TEL

FAX

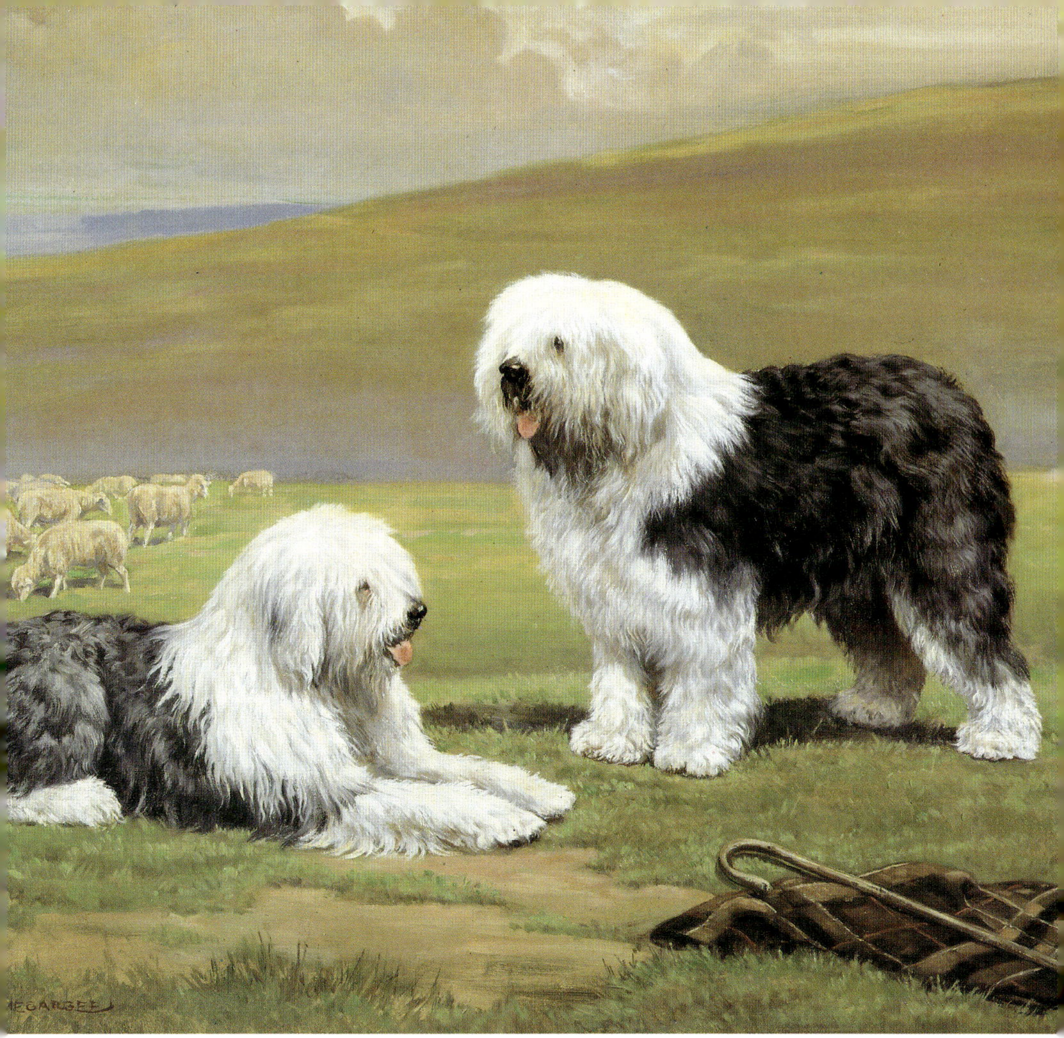

Old English Sheepdogs, 20th century, Edwin Megargee.

NAME

ADDRESS

TEL

FAX

NAME

ADDRESS

TEL

FAX

H

NAME

ADDRESS

TEL

FAX

NAME

ADDRESS

TEL

FAX

NAME

ADDRESS

TEL

FAX

NAME

ADDRESS

TEL

FAX

NAME

ADDRESS

TEL

FAX

NAME

ADDRESS

TEL

FAX

H

NAME

ADDRESS

TEL

FAX

NAME

ADDRESS

TEL

FAX

NAME

ADDRESS

TEL

FAX

NAME

ADDRESS

TEL

FAX

NAME

ADDRESS

TEL

FAX

NAME

ADDRESS

TEL

FAX

H

NAME

ADDRESS

TEL

FAX

NAME

ADDRESS

TEL

FAX

NAME

ADDRESS

TEL

FAX

NAME

ADDRESS

TEL

FAX

NAME

ADDRESS

TEL

FAX

NAME

ADDRESS

TEL

FAX

King Charles Spaniels, Richard Ansdell.

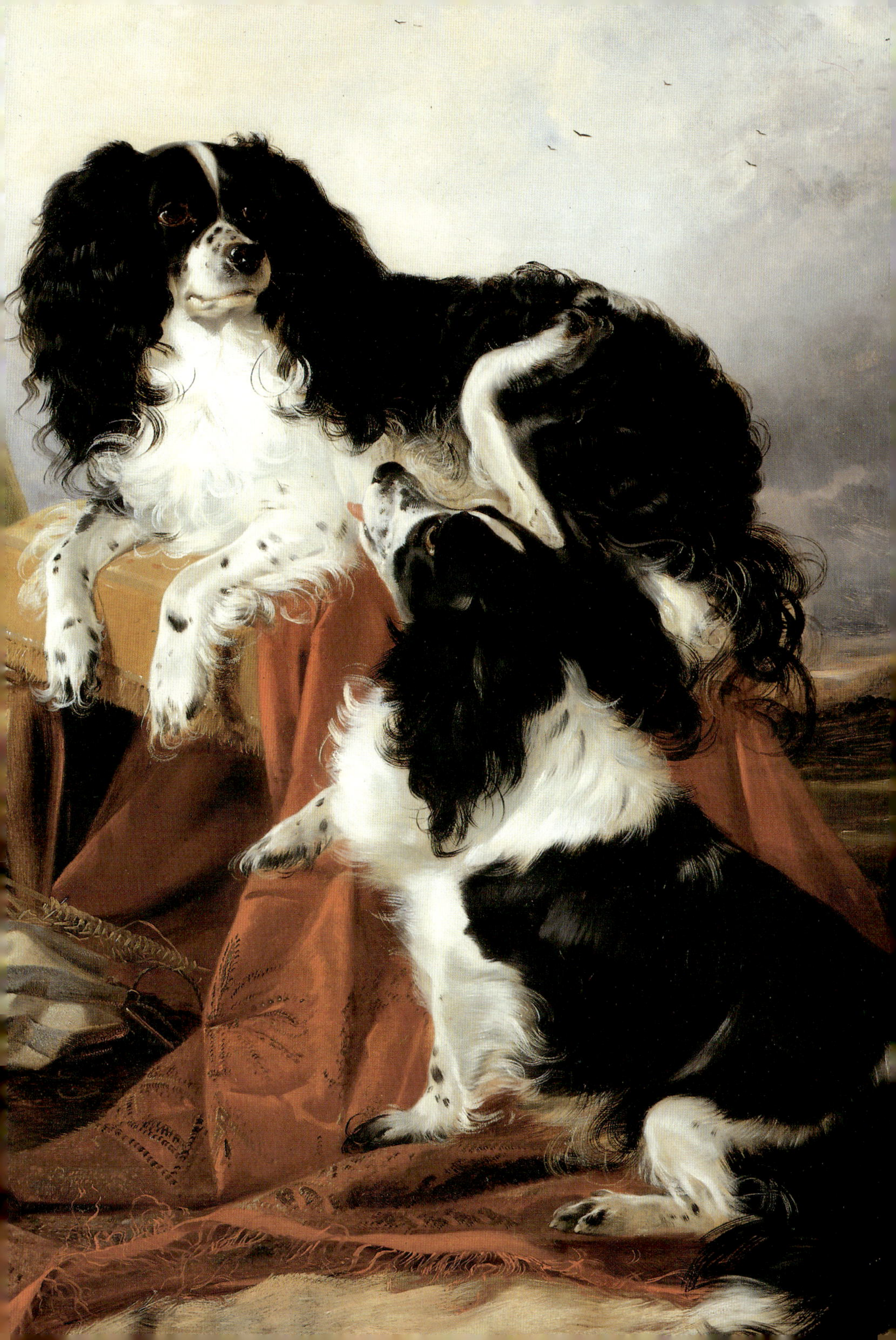

H

NAME

ADDRESS

TEL

FAX

NAME

ADDRESS

TEL

FAX

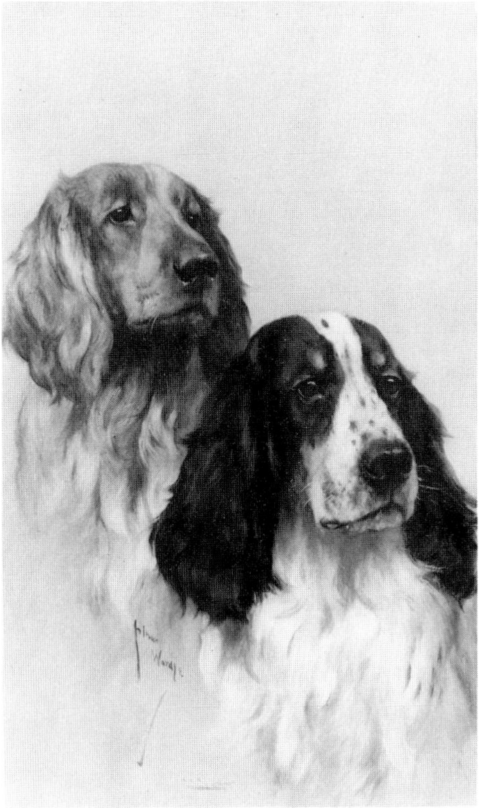

Springer Spaniels, c.1900, Arthur Wardle.

NAME

ADDRESS

TEL

FAX

NAME

ADDRESS

TEL

FAX

H

With eye upraised his master's look to scan; The joy, the solace, and the aid of man. Anon.

NAME ....

....

ADDRESS ....

....

....

....

TEL ....

....

FAX ....

NAME ....

....

ADDRESS ....

....

....

....

TEL ....

....

FAX ....

NAME ....

....

ADDRESS ....

....

....

....

TEL ....

....

FAX ....

NAME ....

....

ADDRESS ....

....

....

....

TEL ....

....

FAX ....

NAME ....

....

ADDRESS ....

....

....

....

TEL ....

....

FAX ....

NAME ....

....

ADDRESS ....

....

....

....

TEL ....

....

FAX ....

I

Half the handsome spaniels in England are called Dash, just as half the tall footmen are called Thomas. M.R. Mitford

NAME ....

....

ADDRESS ....

....

....

....

TEL ....

....

FAX ....

NAME ....

....

ADDRESS ....

....

....

....

TEL ....

....

FAX ....

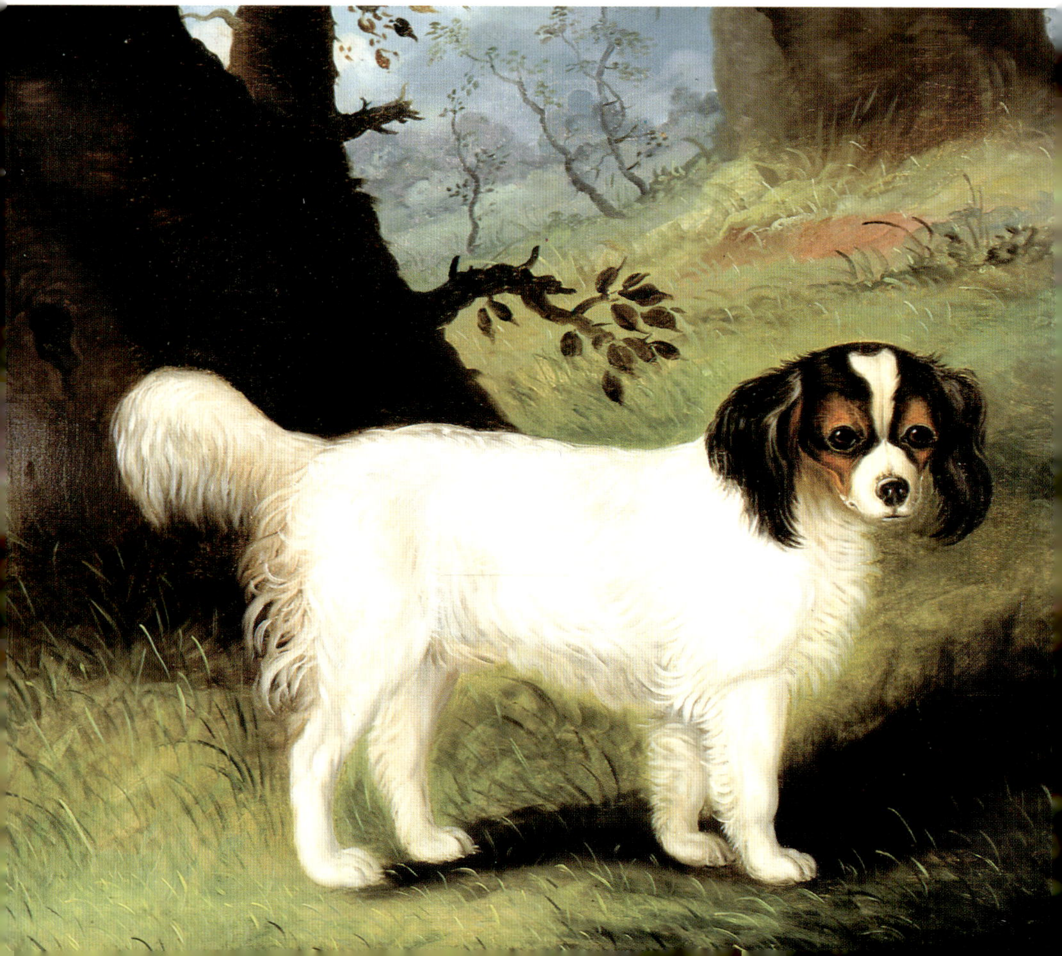

NAME

ADDRESS

TEL

FAX

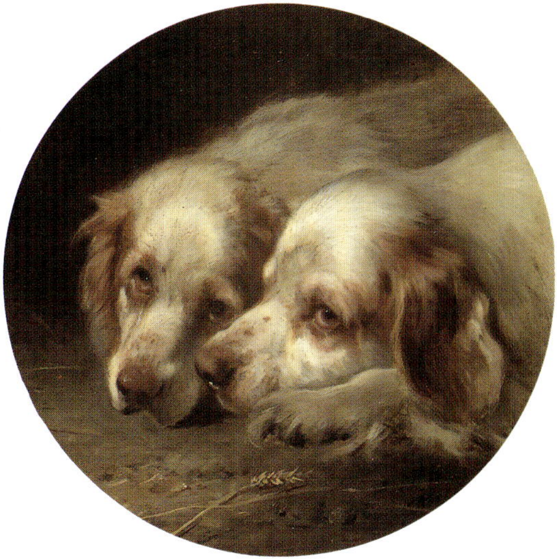

Spaniels, Thomas Earl.

NAME

ADDRESS

TEL

FAX

NAME

ADDRESS

TEL

FAX

NAME

ADDRESS

TEL

FAX

NAME

ADDRESS

TEL

FAX

King Charles Spaniel, 1835, Samuel Spode.

I

NAME
ADDRESS
TEL
FAX

NAME
ADDRESS
TEL
FAX

NAME
ADDRESS
TEL
FAX

NAME
ADDRESS
TEL
FAX

NAME
ADDRESS
TEL
FAX

NAME
ADDRESS
TEL
FAX

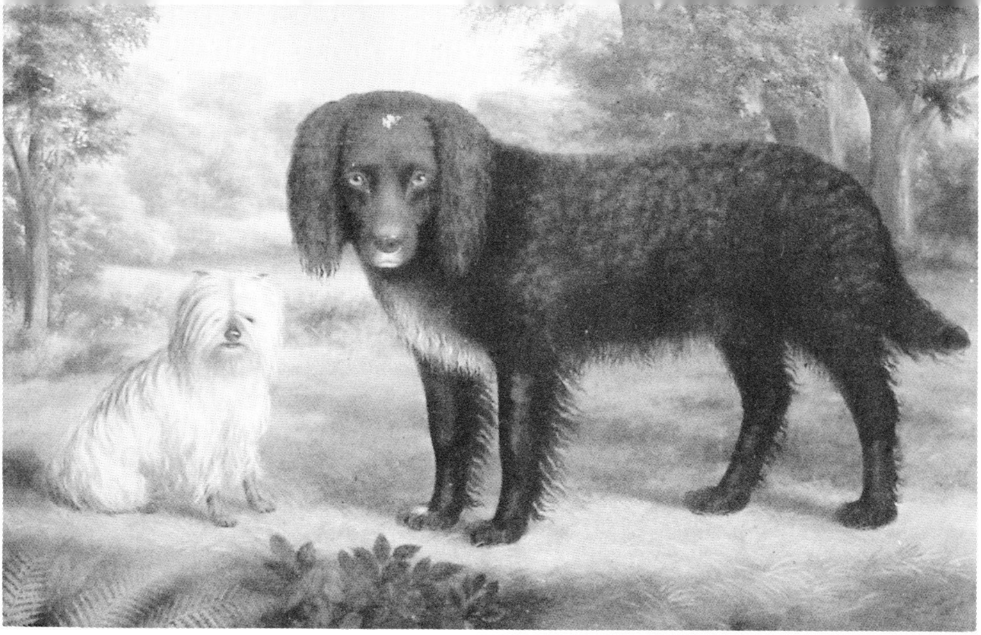

NAME

ADDRESS

TEL

FAX

NAME

ADDRESS

TEL

FAX

NAME

ADDRESS

TEL

FAX

NAME

ADDRESS

TEL

FAX

Spaniel and Toy Terrier, late 19th century.

J

The Dog toils not, neither does he spin, yet Solomon in all his glory never lay upon a doormat all day long. . . while his master worked for the means wherewith to purchase an idle wag of the Solomonic tail. Ambrose Bierce

NAME ....

....

ADDRESS ....

....

....

....

TEL ....

....

FAX ....

NAME ....

....

ADDRESS ....

....

....

....

TEL ....

....

FAX ....

NAME ....

....

ADDRESS ....

....

....

....

TEL ....

....

FAX ....

NAME ....

....

ADDRESS ....

....

....

....

TEL ....

....

FAX ....

NAME ....

....

ADDRESS ....

....

....

....

TEL ....

....

FAX ....

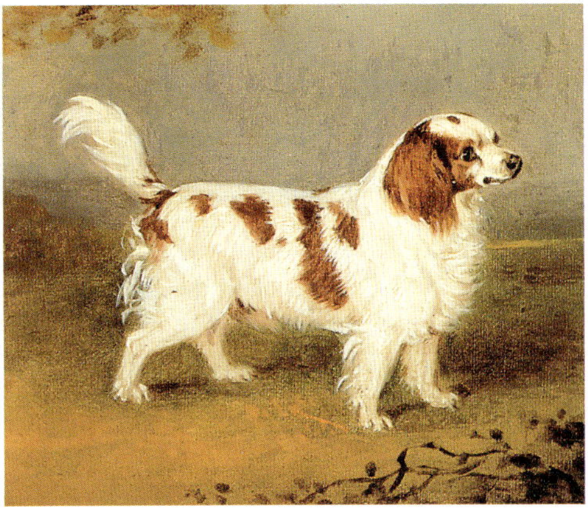

Blenheim King Charles Spaniel, 1816, Henry Bernard Chalon.

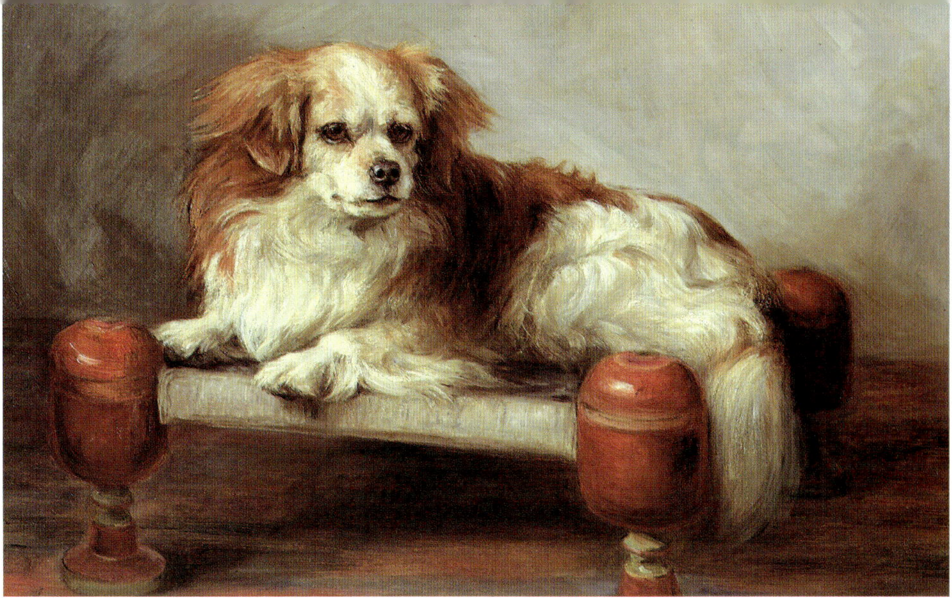

Tibetan Spaniel, 1915. Florence Jay.

NAME ....

....

ADDRESS ....

....

....

....

TEL ....

....

FAX ....

NAME ....

....

ADDRESS ....

....

....

....

TEL ....

....

FAX ....

NAME ....

....

ADDRESS ....

....

....

....

TEL ....

....

FAX ....

NAME ....

....

ADDRESS ....

....

....

....

TEL ....

....

FAX ....

J

NAME

ADDRESS

TEL

FAX

NAME

ADDRESS

TEL

FAX

NAME

ADDRESS

TEL

FAX

NAME

ADDRESS

TEL

FAX

NAME

ADDRESS

TEL

FAX

NAME

ADDRESS

TEL

FAX

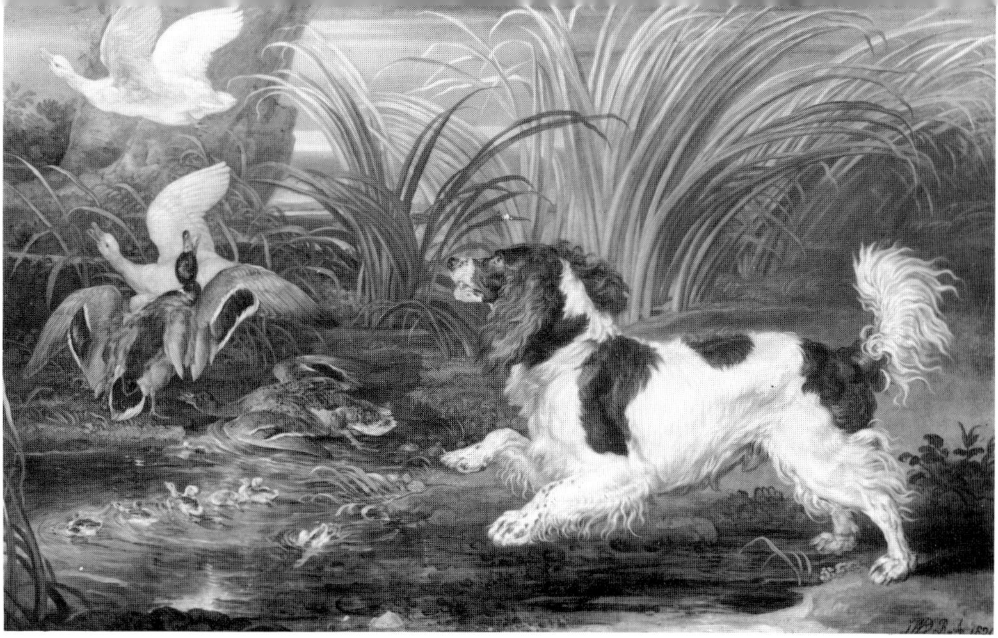

NAME

ADDRESS

TEL

FAX

NAME

ADDRESS

TEL

FAX

NAME

ADDRESS

TEL

FAX

NAME

ADDRESS

TEL

FAX

Spaniel, 1821, James Ward.

J

NAME

ADDRESS

TEL

FAX

NAME

ADDRESS

TEL

FAX

NAME

ADDRESS

TEL

FAX

NAME

ADDRESS

TEL

FAX

NAME

ADDRESS

TEL

FAX

NAME

ADDRESS

TEL

FAX

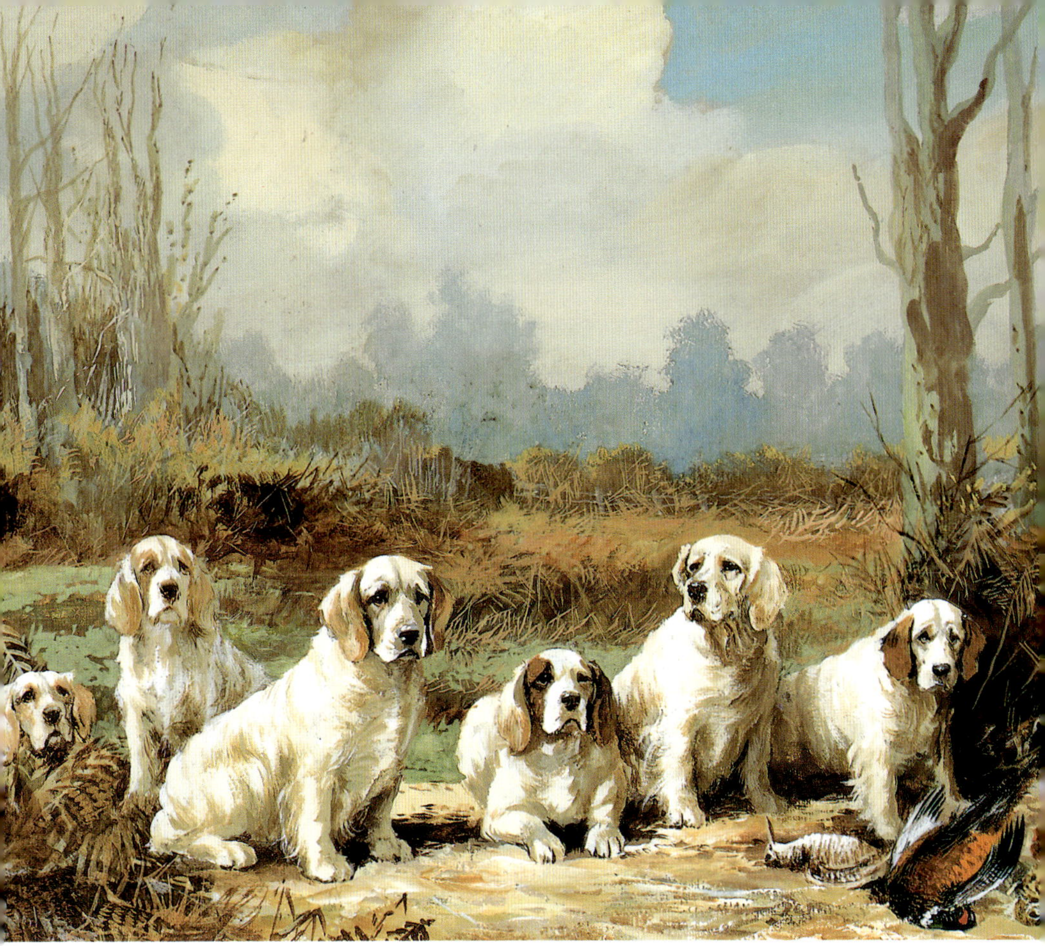

Clumber Spaniels, 1930, Reuben Ward Binks

NAME ....

....

ADDRESS ....

....

....

....

TEL ....

....

FAX ....

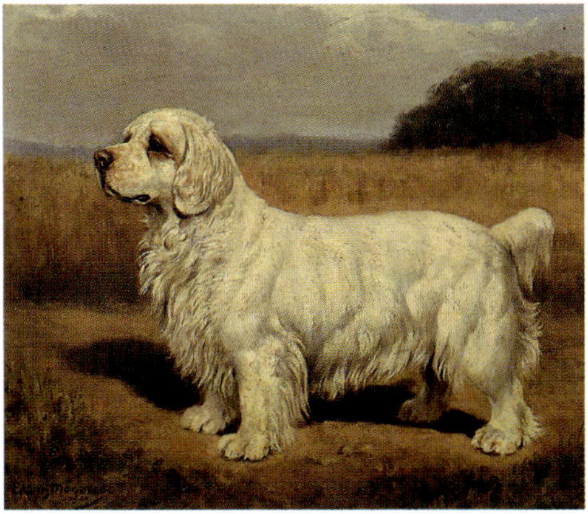

Clumber Spaniel, 1944, Edwin Megargee.

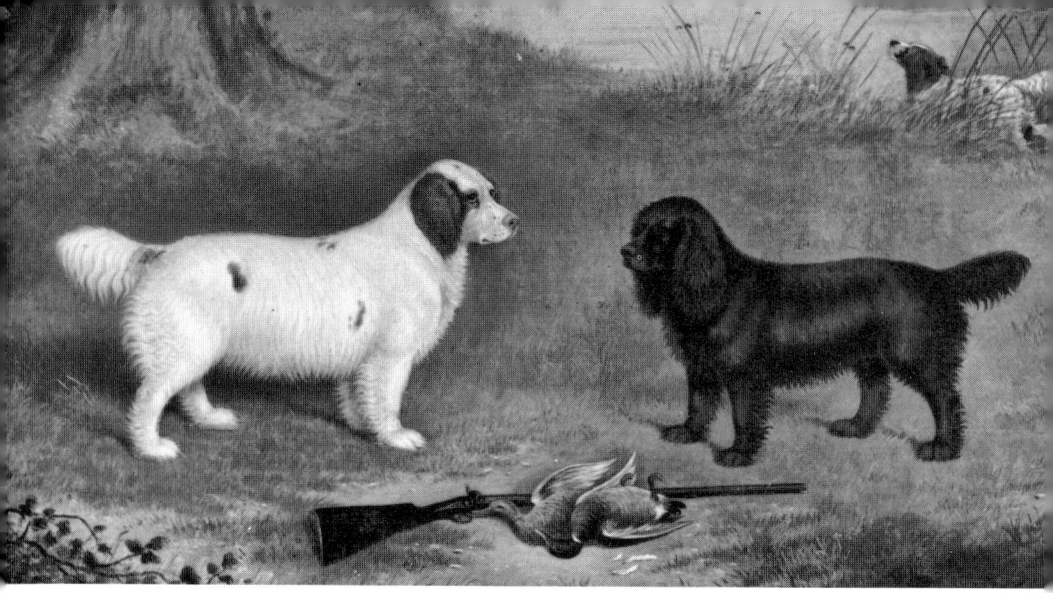

Spaniels, 1868, William E. Turner.

NAME

ADDRESS

TEL

FAX

NAME

ADDRESS

TEL

FAX

NAME

ADDRESS

TEL

FAX

NAME

ADDRESS

TEL

FAX

K

NAME

ADDRESS

TEL

FAX

NAME

ADDRESS

TEL

FAX

NAME

ADDRESS

TEL

FAX

NAME

ADDRESS

TEL

FAX

NAME

ADDRESS

TEL

FAX

NAME

ADDRESS

TEL

FAX

K

Poodles always listen attentively while being scolded, looking innocent, bewildered, and misunderstood. James Thurber

NAME ....

....

ADDRESS ....

....

....

....

TEL ....

....

FAX ....

NAME ....

....

ADDRESS ....

....

....

....

TEL ....

....

FAX ....

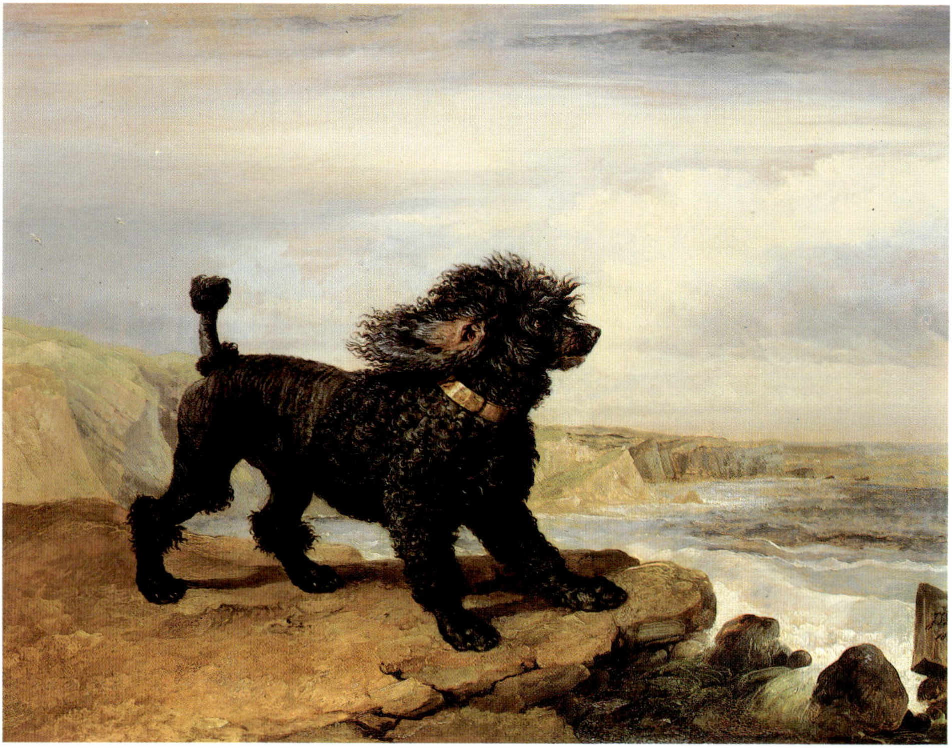

Poodle, 1812, James Ward.

NAME ....

ADDRESS ....

TEL ....

FAX ....

NAME ....

ADDRESS ....

TEL ....

FAX ....

NAME ....

ADDRESS ....

TEL ....

FAX ....

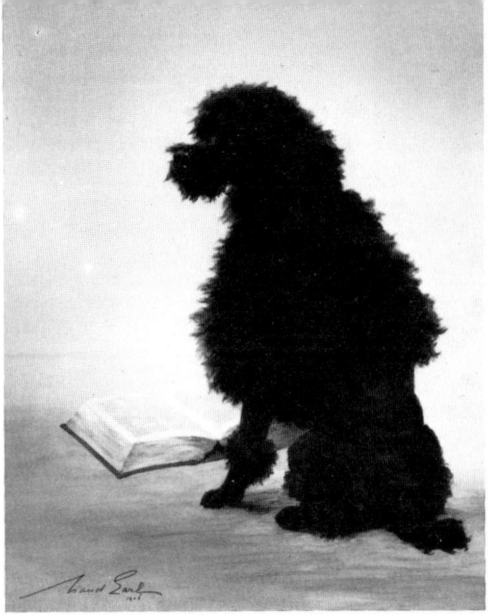

Poodle, 1906, Maud Earl.

NAME ....

ADDRESS ....

TEL ....

FAX ....

NAME ....

ADDRESS ....

TEL ....

FAX ....

K

NAME

ADDRESS

TEL

FAX

NAME

ADDRESS

TEL

FAX

NAME

ADDRESS

TEL

FAX

NAME

ADDRESS

TEL

FAX

NAME

ADDRESS

TEL

FAX

NAME

ADDRESS

TEL

FAX

K

NAME ....

....

ADDRESS ....

....

....

....

TEL ....

....

FAX ....

NAME ....

....

ADDRESS ....

....

....

....

TEL ....

....

FAX ....

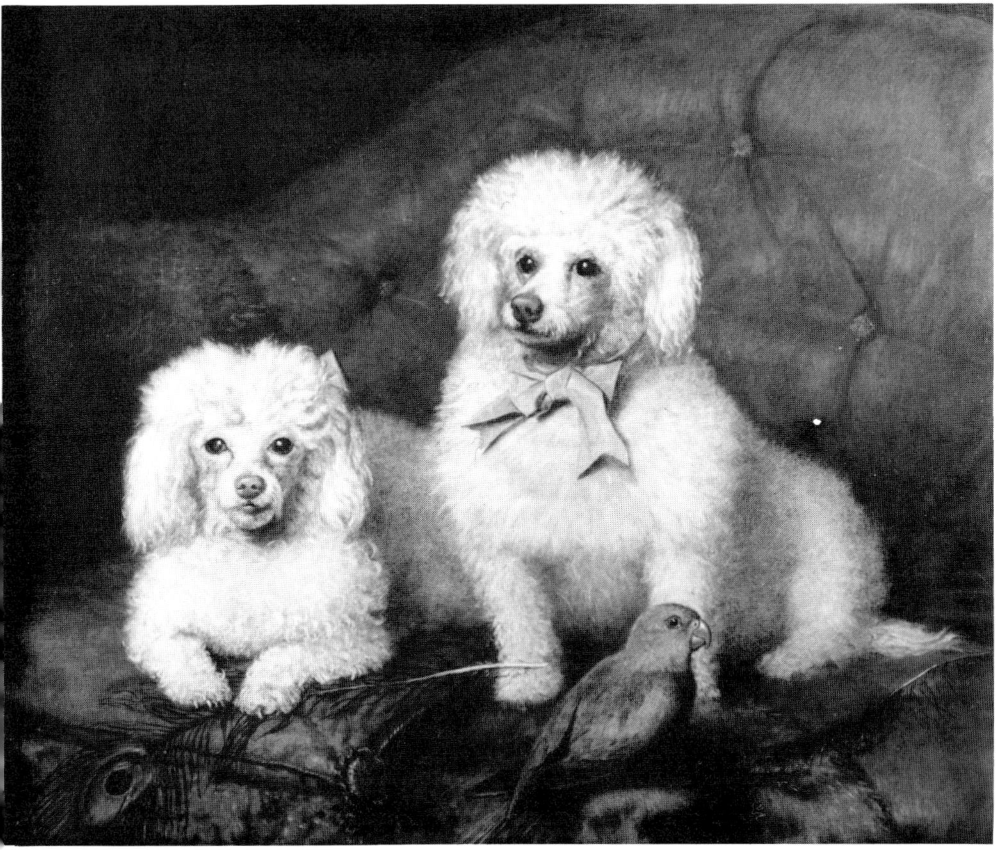

Poodles, 1858, John Watkins Chapman.

L

Charley was born on the outskirts of Paris and trained in France, and while he knows a little poodle-English, he responds quickly only to commands in French. Otherwise he has to translate, and that slows him down. John Steinbeck

NAME

ADDRESS

TEL

FAX

NAME

ADDRESS

TEL

FAX

NAME

ADDRESS

TEL

FAX

NAME

ADDRESS

TEL

FAX

NAME

ADDRESS

TEL

FAX

NAME

ADDRESS

TEL

FAX

Poodle, 1867, J. Jack.

L

NAME ....

....

ADDRESS ....

....

....

....

TEL ....

....

FAX ....

NAME ....

....

ADDRESS ....

....

....

....

TEL ....

....

FAX ....

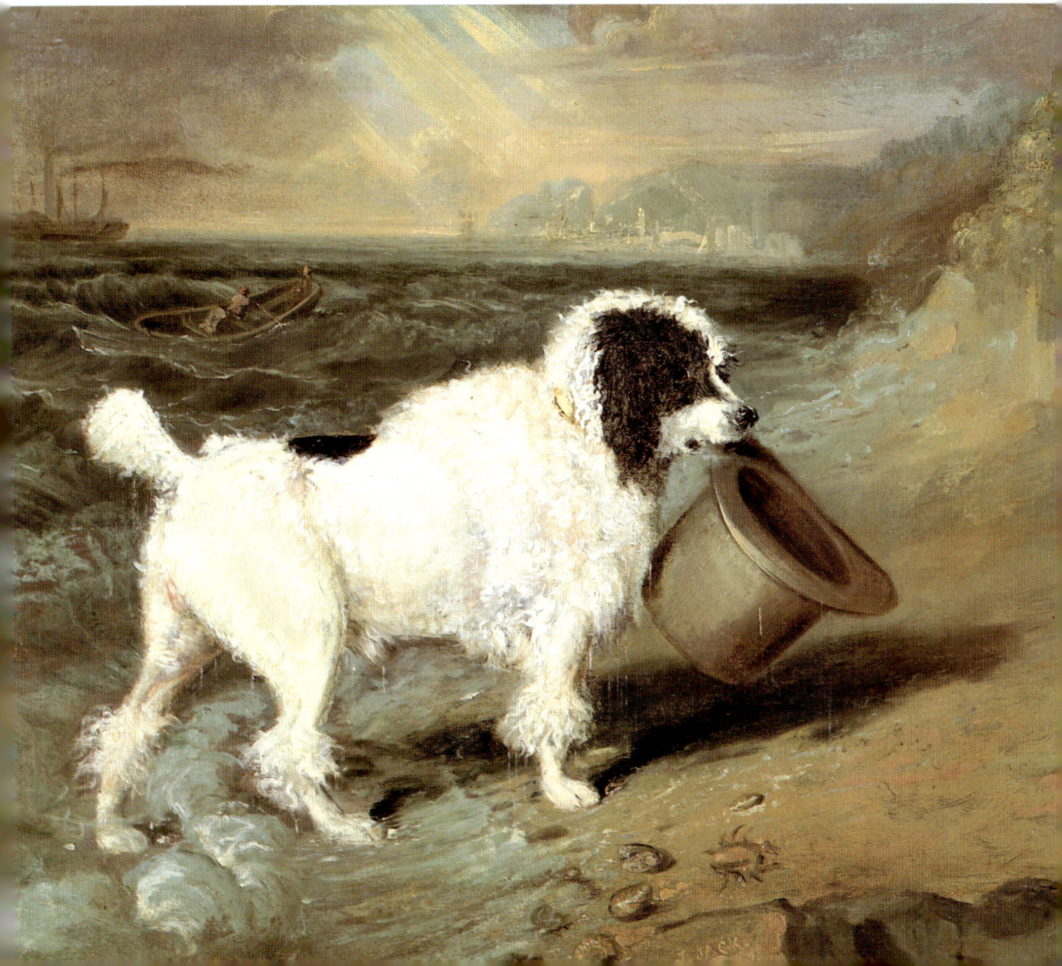

L

Dogs laugh, but they laugh with their tails Max Eastman

NAME ....

....

ADDRESS ....

....

....

....

TEL ....

....

FAX ....

NAME ....

....

ADDRESS ....

....

....

....

TEL ....

....

FAX ....

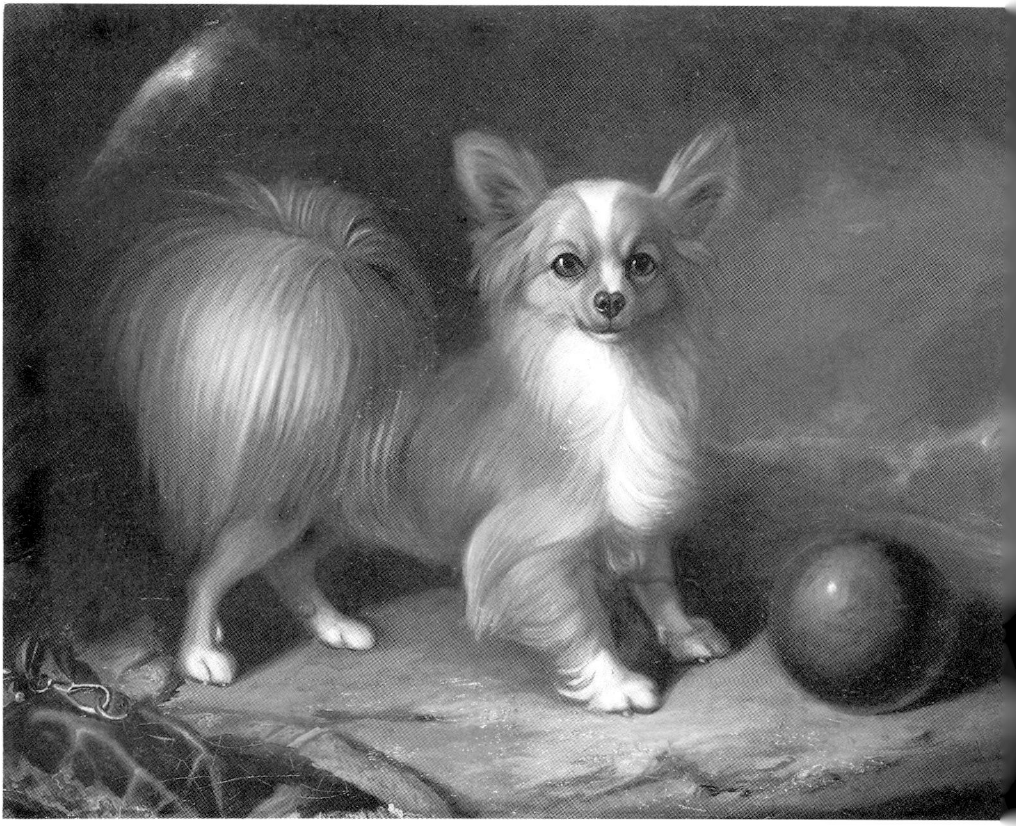

Papillon, 1893, Malcolm S. Tucker.

L

NAME

ADDRESS

TEL

FAX

NAME

ADDRESS

TEL

FAX

NAME

ADDRESS

TEL

FAX

NAME

ADDRESS

TEL

FAX

NAME

ADDRESS

TEL

FAX

NAME

ADDRESS

TEL

FAX

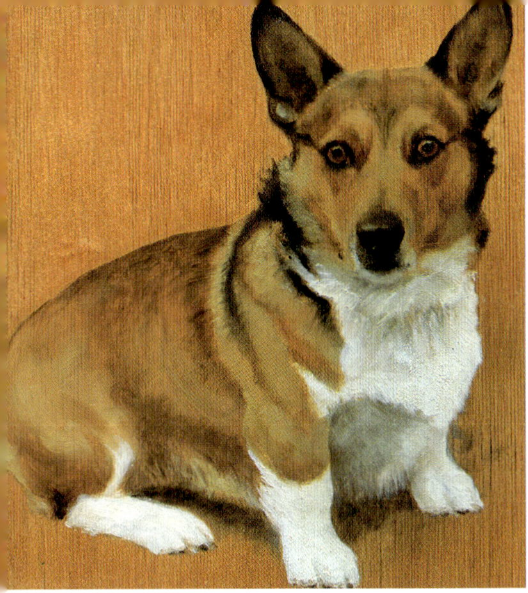

Corgi, Florence Mabel Hollams.

NAME ....

ADDRESS ....

TEL ....

FAX ....

NAME ....

ADDRESS ....

TEL ....

FAX ....

NAME ....

ADDRESS ....

TEL ....

FAX ....

NAME ....

ADDRESS ....

TEL ....

FAX ....

NAME ....

ADDRESS ....

TEL ....

FAX ....

West Highland White Terrier, King Charles Spaniel and Cairn Terrier, 1856, George W. Horlor.

L

NAME

ADDRESS

TEL

FAX

NAME

ADDRESS

TEL

FAX

NAME

ADDRESS

TEL

FAX

NAME

ADDRESS

TEL

FAX

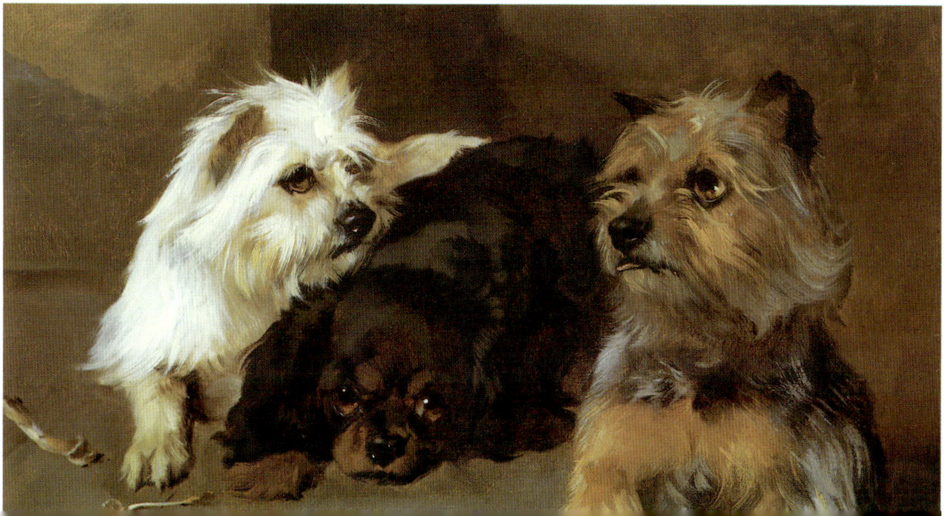

M

NAME

ADDRESS

TEL

FAX

NAME

ADDRESS

TEL

FAX

NAME

ADDRESS

TEL

FAX

NAME

ADDRESS

TEL

FAX

NAME

ADDRESS

TEL

FAX

NAME

ADDRESS

TEL

FAX

M

NAME

ADDRESS

TEL

FAX

NAME

ADDRESS

TEL

FAX

NAME

ADDRESS

TEL

FAX

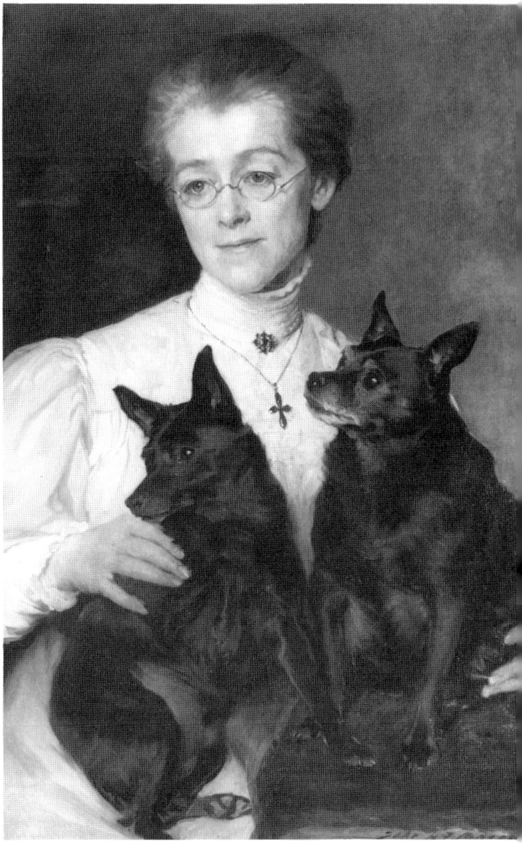

Schipperkes, c.1890, John Henry Frederick Bacon.

NAME

ADDRESS

TEL

FAX

M

NAME

ADDRESS

TEL

FAX

NAME

ADDRESS

TEL

FAX

NAME

ADDRESS

TEL

FAX

NAME

ADDRESS

TEL

FAX

NAME

ADDRESS

TEL

FAX

NAME

ADDRESS

TEL

FAX

Dogs are superior to human beings as companions. They do not quarrel or argue with you. They never talk about themselves but listen to you while you talk about yourself, and keep up an appearance of being interested in the conversation. Jerome K. Jerome

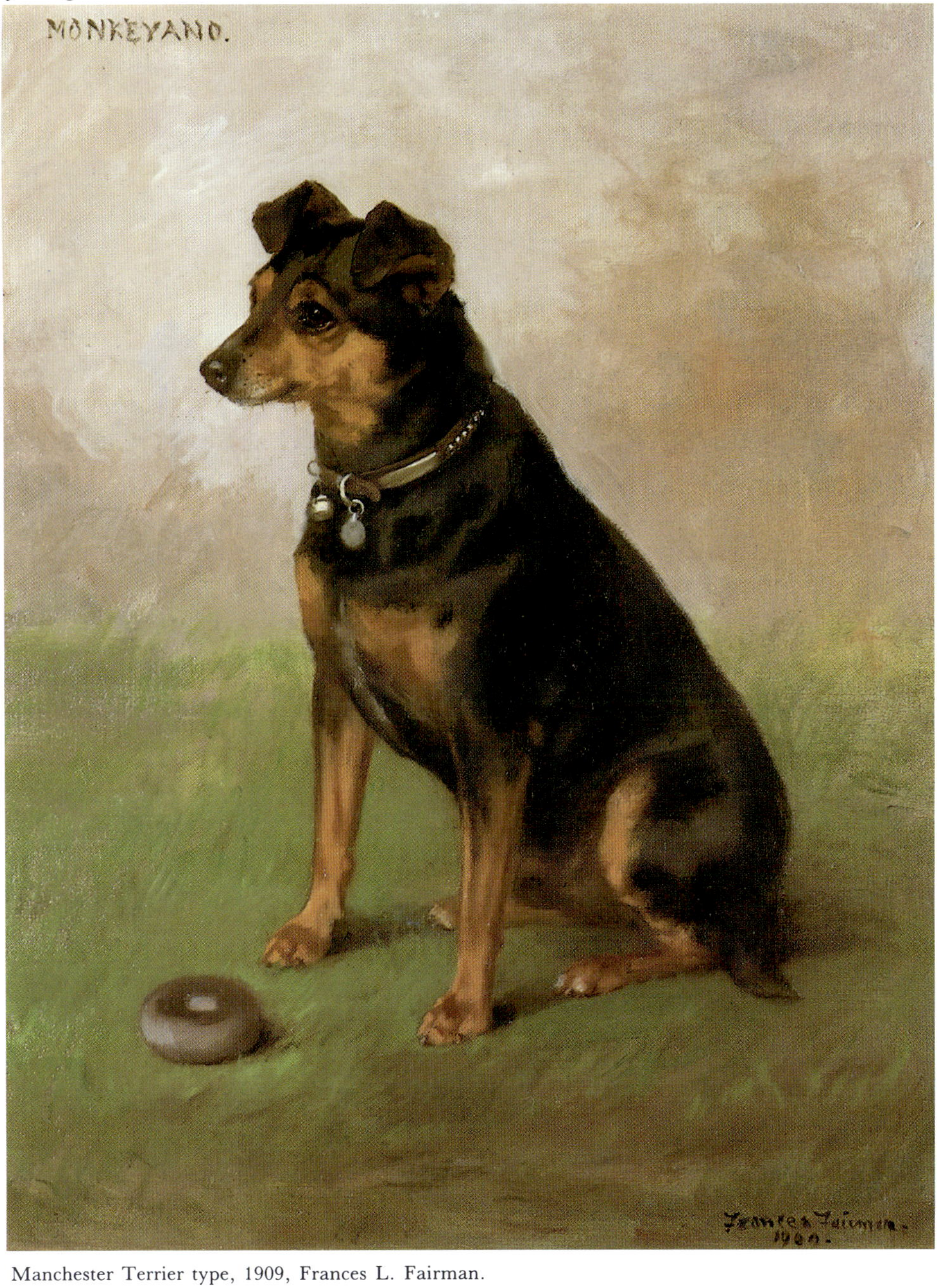

Manchester Terrier type, 1909, Frances L. Fairman.

M

If you pick up a starving dog and make him prosperous he will not bite you. Mark Twain

NAME ....

....

ADDRESS ....

....

....

....

TEL ....

....

FAX ....

NAME ....

....

ADDRESS ....

....

....

....

TEL ....

....

FAX ....

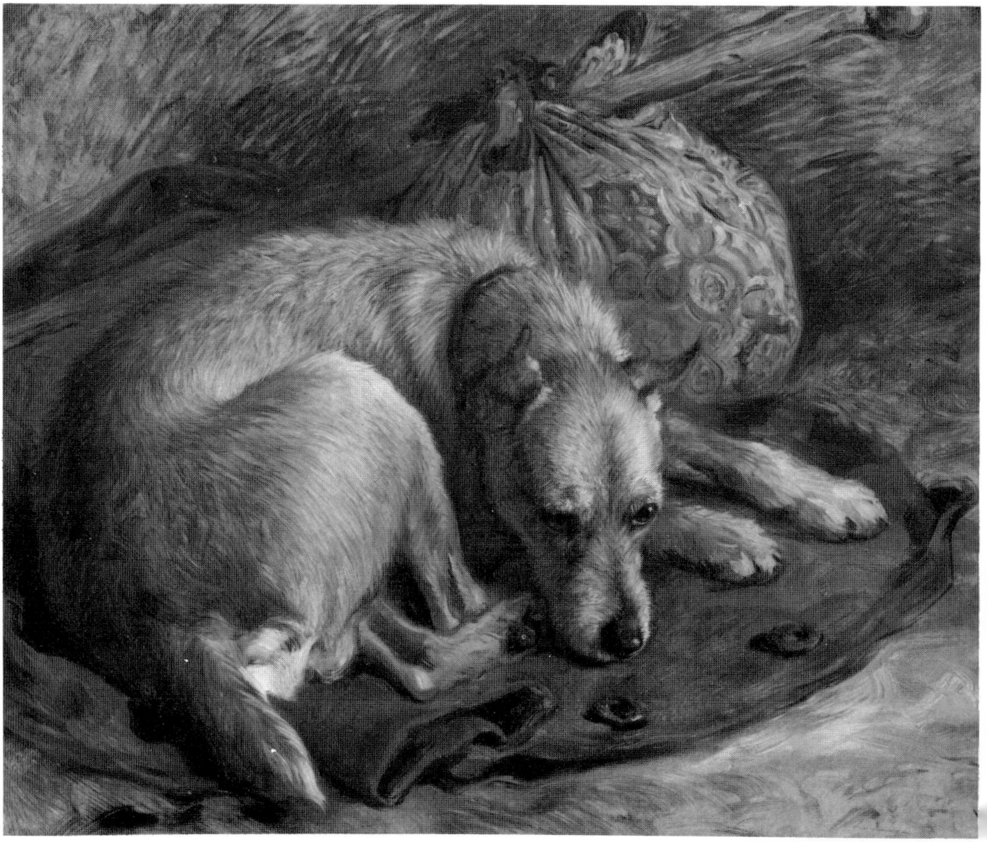

Irish Terrier, 1884, Frank Paton.

M

NAME

ADDRESS

TEL

FAX

NAME

ADDRESS

TEL

FAX

NAME

ADDRESS

TEL

FAX

NAME

ADDRESS

TEL

FAX

NAME

ADDRESS

TEL

FAX

NAME

ADDRESS

TEL

FAX

M

At his feet sat a white-coated, red-eyed dog, who occupied himself in winking at his master with both eyes at the same time. Charles Dickens

NAME ....

....

ADDRESS ....

....

....

....

TEL ....

....

FAX ....

NAME ....

....

ADDRESS ....

....

....

....

TEL ....

....

FAX ....

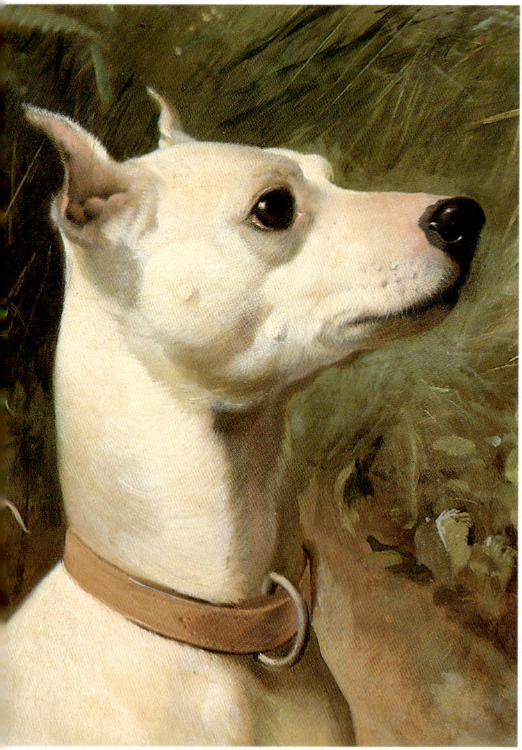

White English Terrier, c.1870, George Earl.

NAME ....

....

ADDRESS ....

....

....

....

TEL ....

....

FAX ....

NAME ....

....

ADDRESS ....

....

....

....

TEL ....

....

FAX ....

White English Terrier, c.1870, George Earl

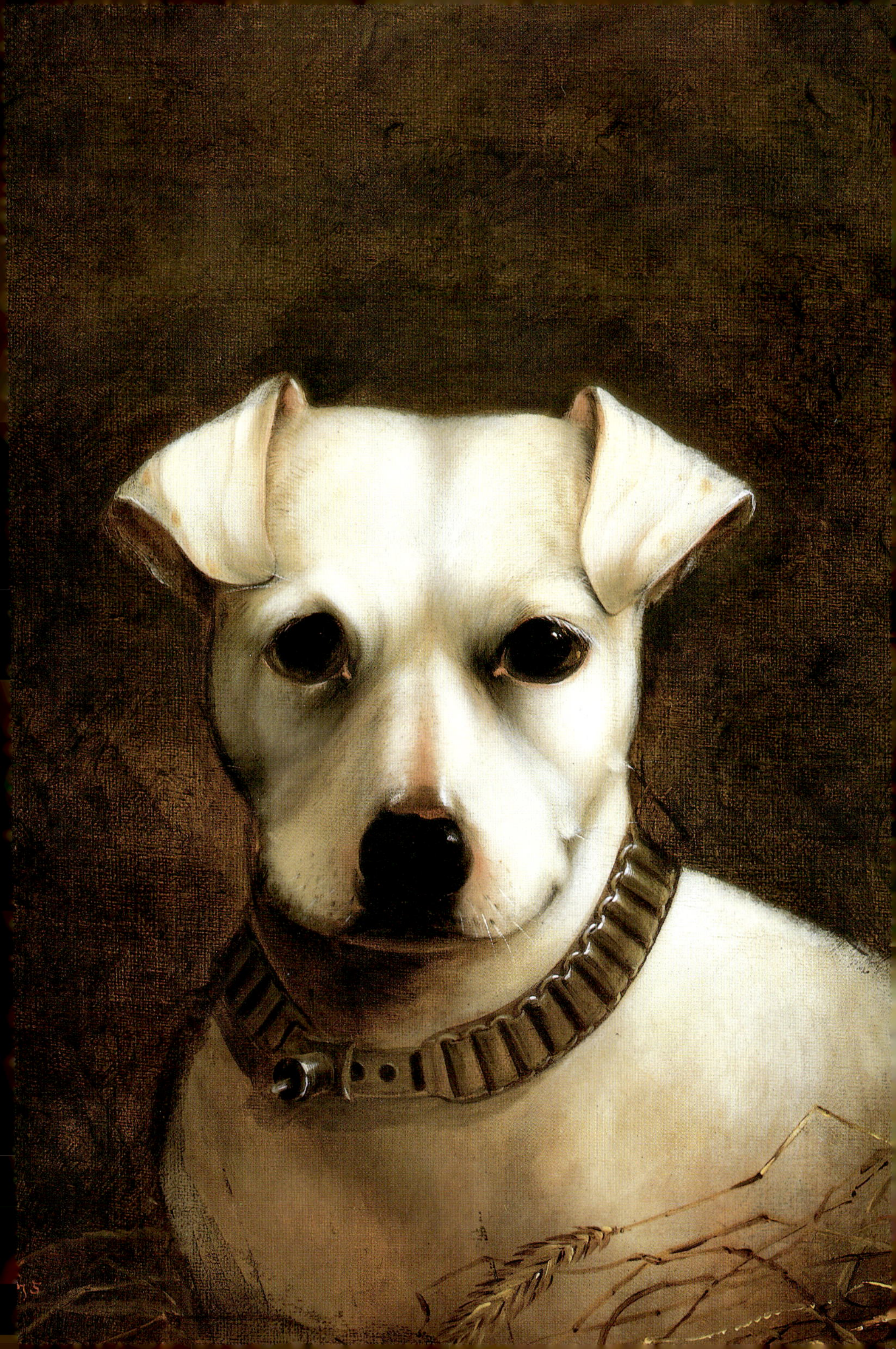

N

NAME

ADDRESS

TEL

FAX

NAME

ADDRESS

TEL

FAX

NAME

ADDRESS

TEL

FAX

NAME

ADDRESS

TEL

FAX

NAME

ADDRESS

TEL

FAX

NAME

ADDRESS

TEL

FAX

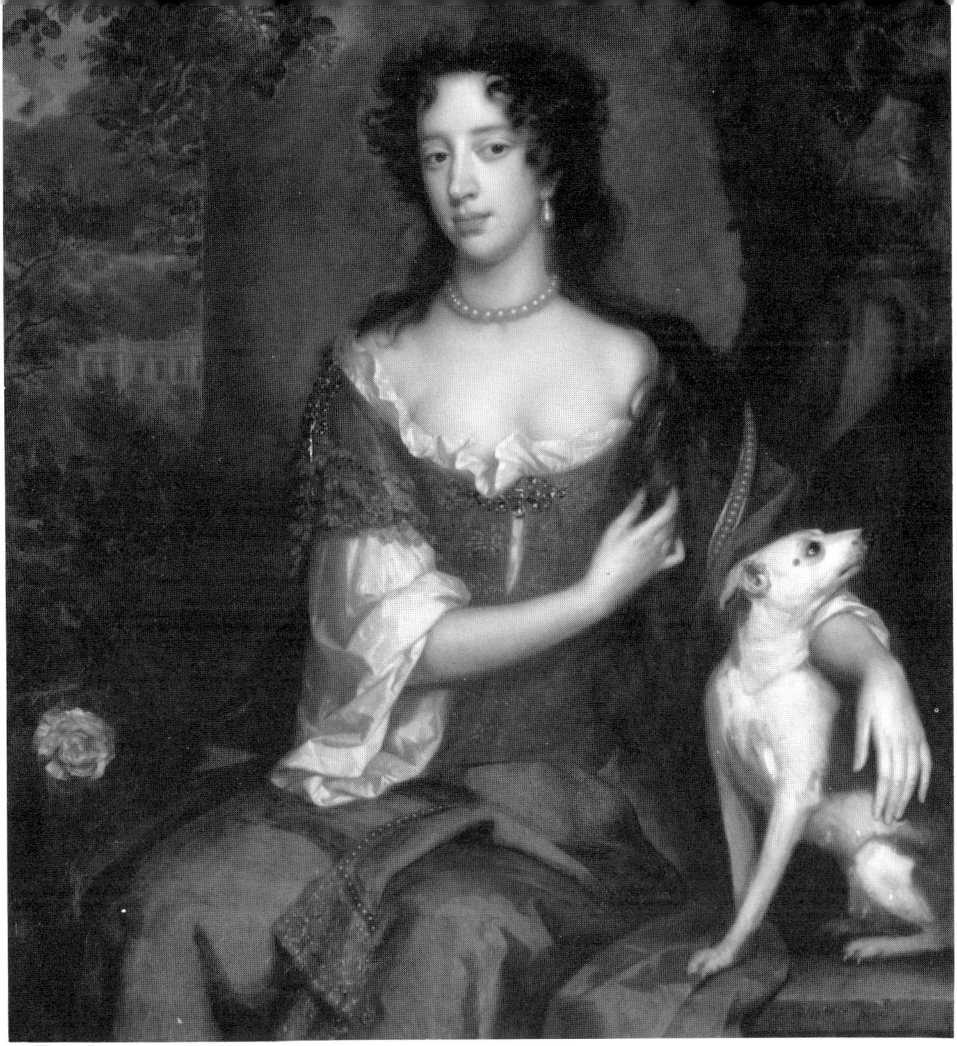

Terrier, c.1685, William Wissing.

NAME ....

....

ADDRESS ....

....

....

....

TEL ....

....

FAX ....

NAME ....

....

ADDRESS ....

....

....

....

TEL ....

....

FAX ....

N

Ceaseless and implacable growls from under the chair indicated the presence of a woolly dog.
Somerville & Ross

NAME ....

....

ADDRESS ....

....

....

....

TEL ....

....

FAX ....

NAME ....

....

ADDRESS ....

....

....

....

TEL ....

....

FAX ....

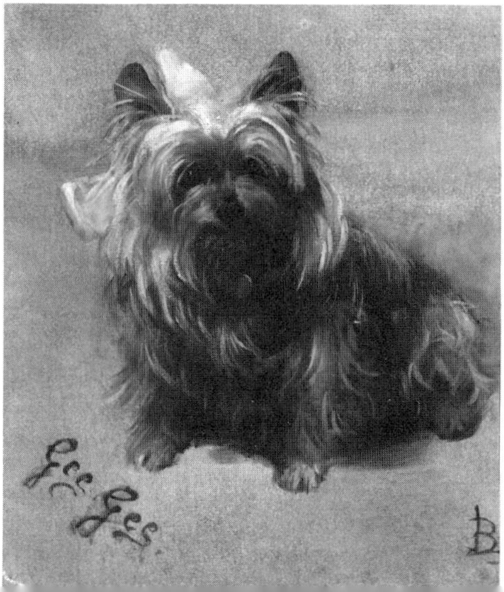

NAME ....

....

ADDRESS ....

....

....

....

TEL ....

....

FAX ....

NAME ....

....

ADDRESS ....

....

....

....

TEL ....

....

FAX ....

NAME ....

....

ADDRESS ....

....

....

....

TEL ....

....

FAX ....

Yorkshire Terrier, English School.

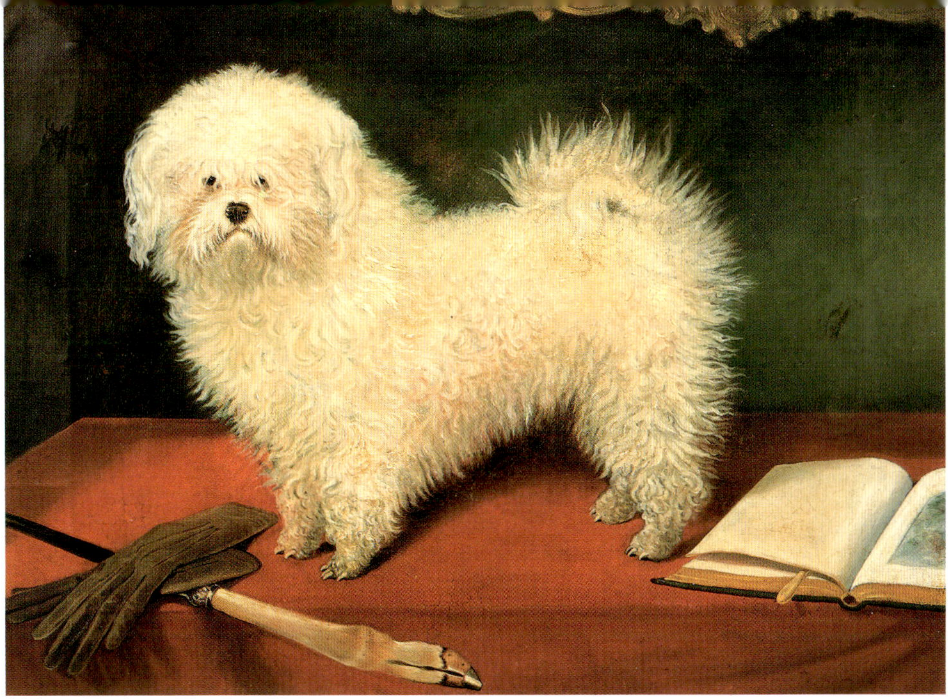
Maltese Terrier, 1881, B.A. Hyland.

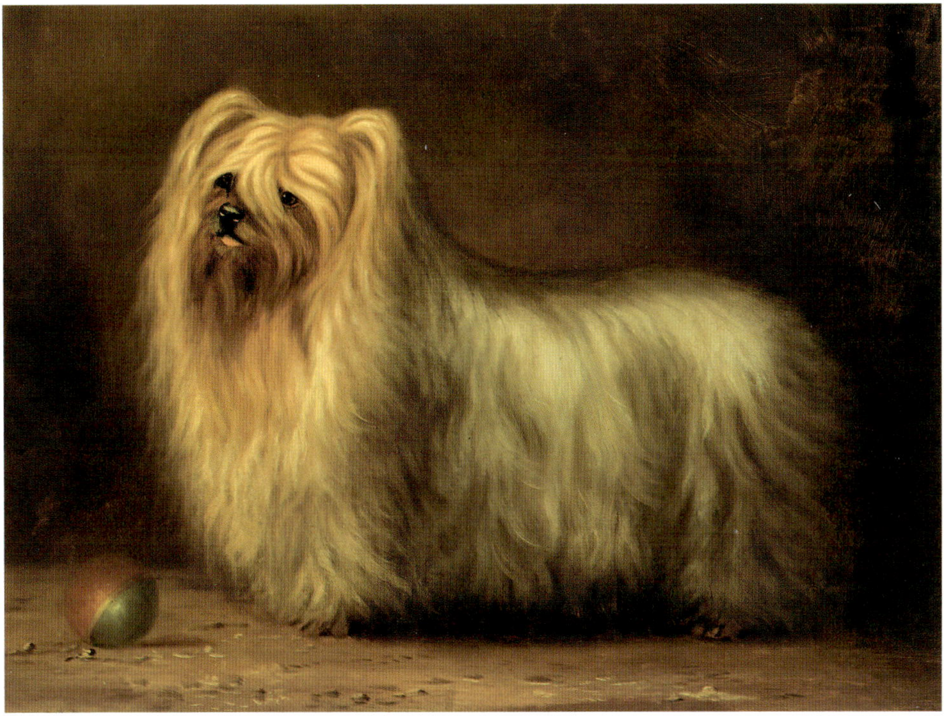
Yorkshire Terrier, English School.

N

Say something idiotic and nobody but a dog politely wags his tail. Virginia Graham

NAME

ADDRESS

TEL

FAX

NAME

ADDRESS

TEL

FAX

NAME

ADDRESS

TEL

FAX

NAME

ADDRESS

TEL

FAX

NAME

ADDRESS

TEL

FAX

NAME

ADDRESS

TEL

FAX

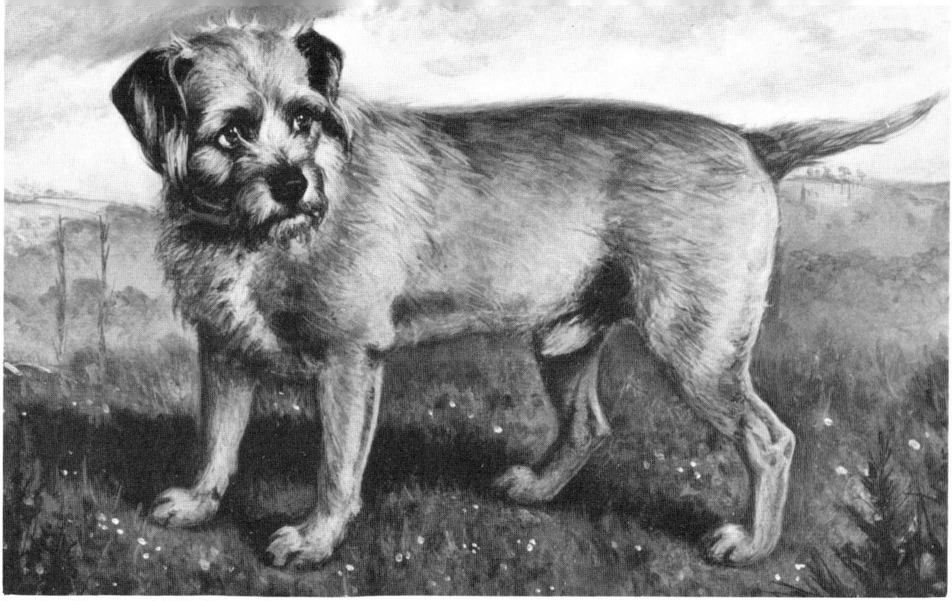

Border Terrier, 1879, W.J. Stevenson.

NAME ....

....

ADDRESS ....

....

....

....

TEL ....

....

FAX ....

NAME ....

....

ADDRESS ....

....

....

....

TEL ....

....

FAX ....

NAME ....

....

ADDRESS ....

....

....

....

TEL ....

....

FAX ....

NAME ....

....

ADDRESS ....

....

....

....

TEL ....

....

FAX ....

O

NAME

ADDRESS

TEL

FAX

NAME

ADDRESS

TEL

FAX

NAME

ADDRESS

TEL

FAX

NAME

ADDRESS

TEL

FAX

NAME

ADDRESS

TEL

FAX

NAME

ADDRESS

TEL

FAX

Wire Fox Terrier and puppies, Arthur Wardle.

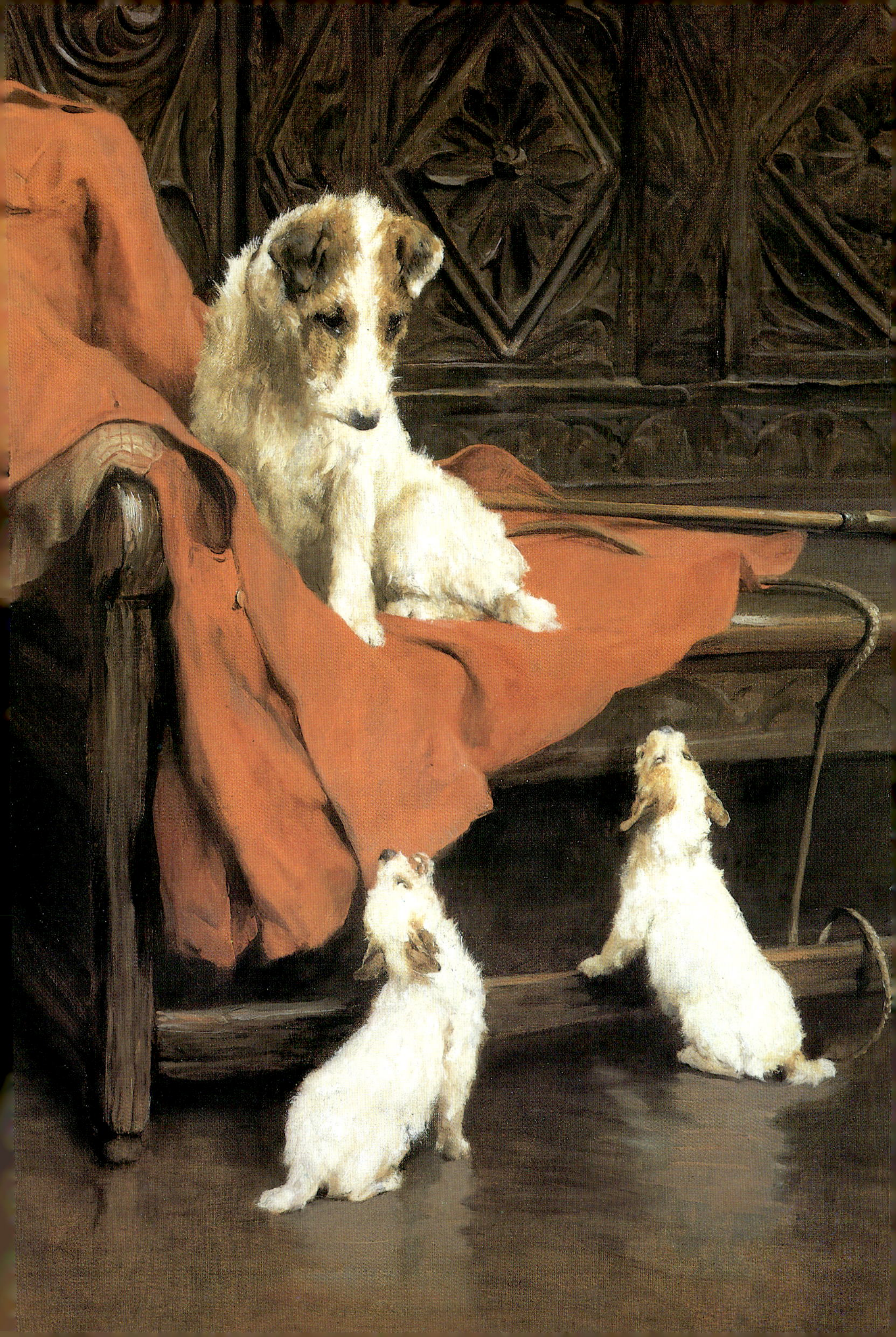

O

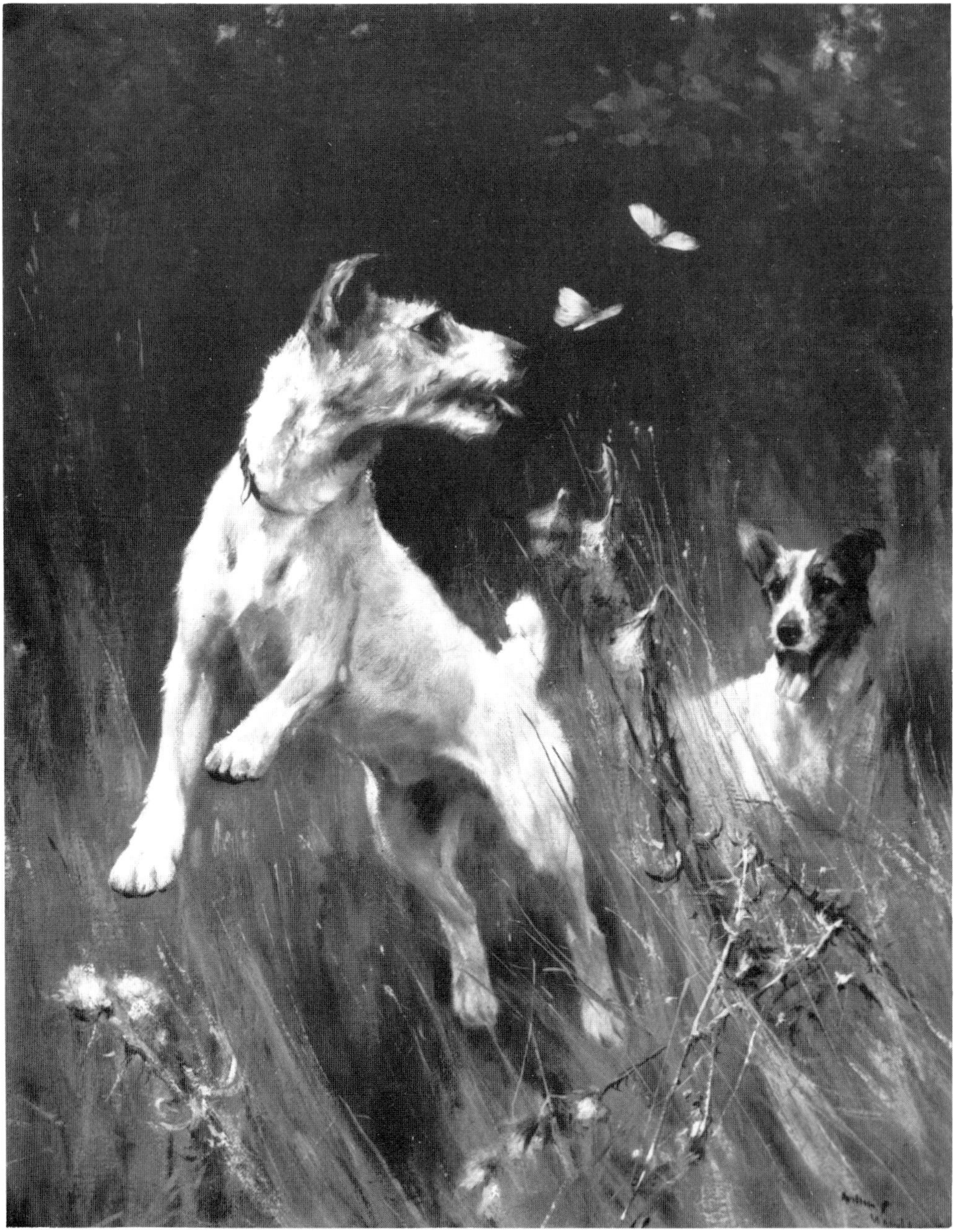

Wire Fox Terriers, c.1900, Arthur Wardle.

To look at Montmerency you would imagine that he was an angel sent upon the earth, for some reason withheld from mankind, in the shape of a small fox-terrier. Jerome K. Jerome

O

NAME

ADDRESS

TEL

FAX

NAME

ADDRESS

TEL

FAX

NAME

ADDRESS

TEL

FAX

NAME

ADDRESS

TEL

FAX

NAME

ADDRESS

TEL

FAX

NAME

ADDRESS

TEL

FAX

P

NAME ....

....

ADDRESS ....

....

....

....

TEL ....

....

FAX ....

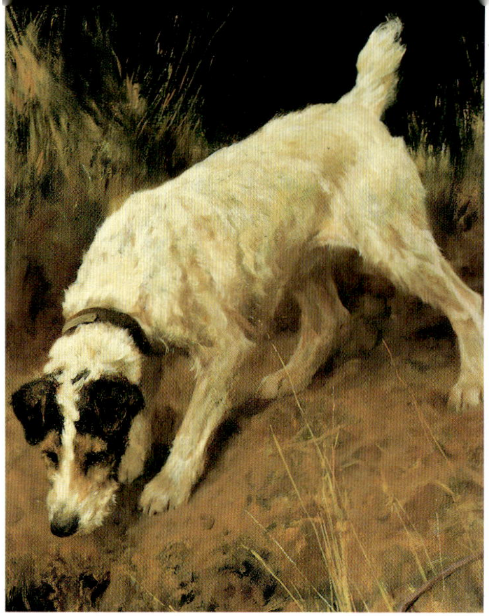

Wire Fox Terrier, Arthur Wardle.

NAME ....

....

ADDRESS ....

....

....

....

TEL ....

....

FAX ....

NAME ....

....

ADDRESS ....

....

....

....

TEL ....

....

FAX ....

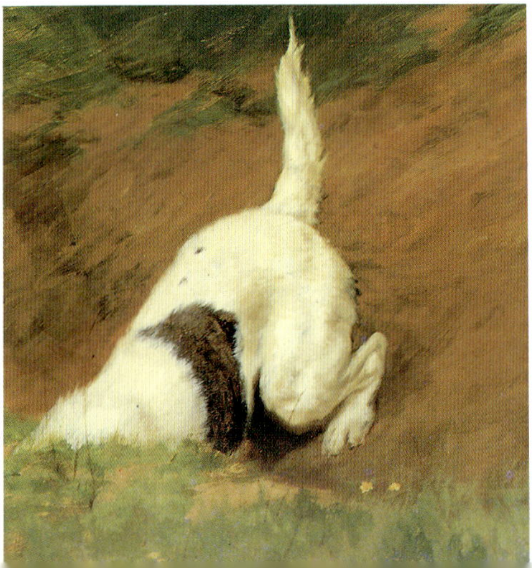

NAME ....

....

ADDRESS ....

....

....

....

TEL ....

....

FAX ....

Smooth Fox Terrier, Maud Earl.

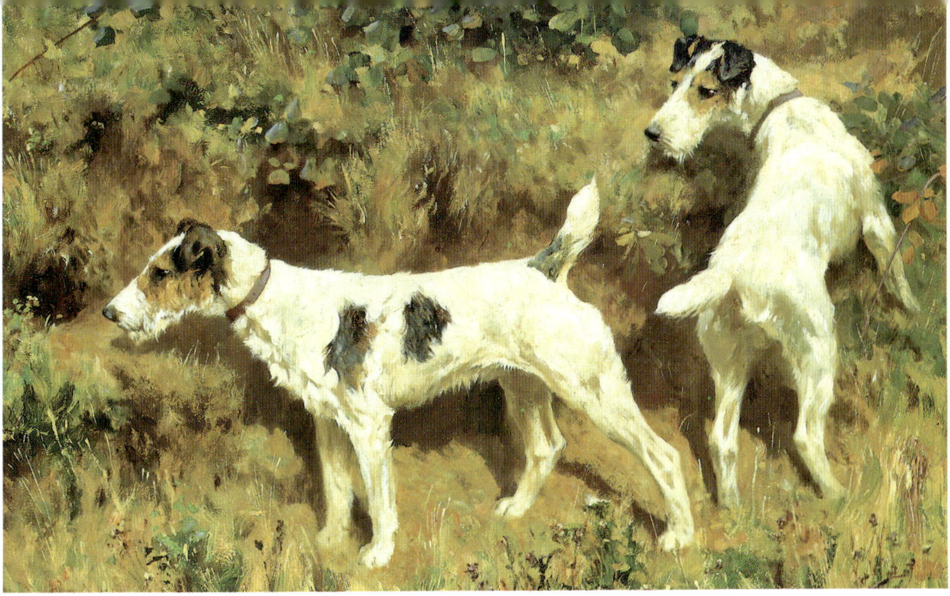

Wire Fox Terriers, Arthur Wardle.

NAME ....

....

ADDRESS ....

....

....

....

TEL ....

....

FAX ....

NAME ....

....

ADDRESS ....

....

....

....

TEL ....

....

FAX ....

NAME ....

....

ADDRESS ....

....

....

....

TEL ....

....

FAX ....

NAME ....

....

ADDRESS ....

....

....

....

TEL ....

....

FAX ....

P

NAME

ADDRESS

TEL

FAX

NAME

ADDRESS

TEL

FAX

NAME

ADDRESS

TEL

FAX

NAME

ADDRESS

TEL

FAX

NAME

ADDRESS

TEL

FAX

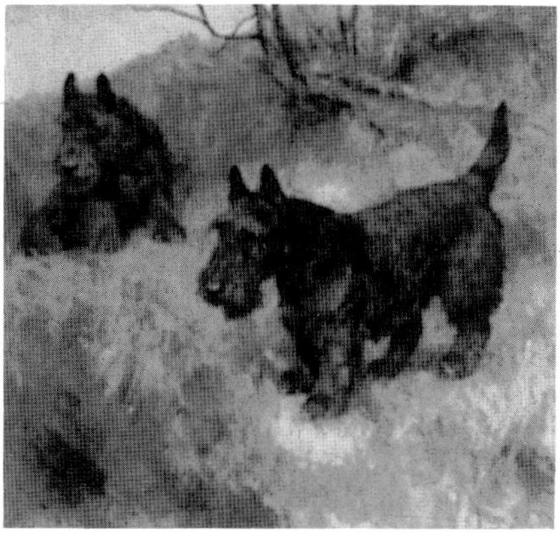

Scottish Terriers, c.1935, Arthur Wardle.

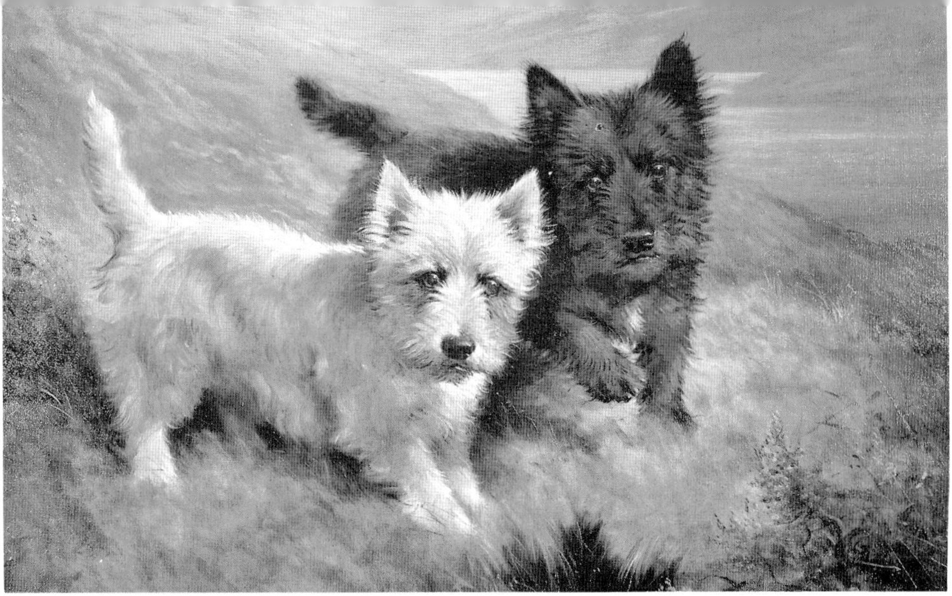

West Highland White and Scottish Terrier, c.1930, Lilian Cheviot.

NAME

ADDRESS

TEL

FAX

NAME

ADDRESS

TEL

FAX

NAME

ADDRESS

TEL

FAX

NAME

ADDRESS

TEL

FAX

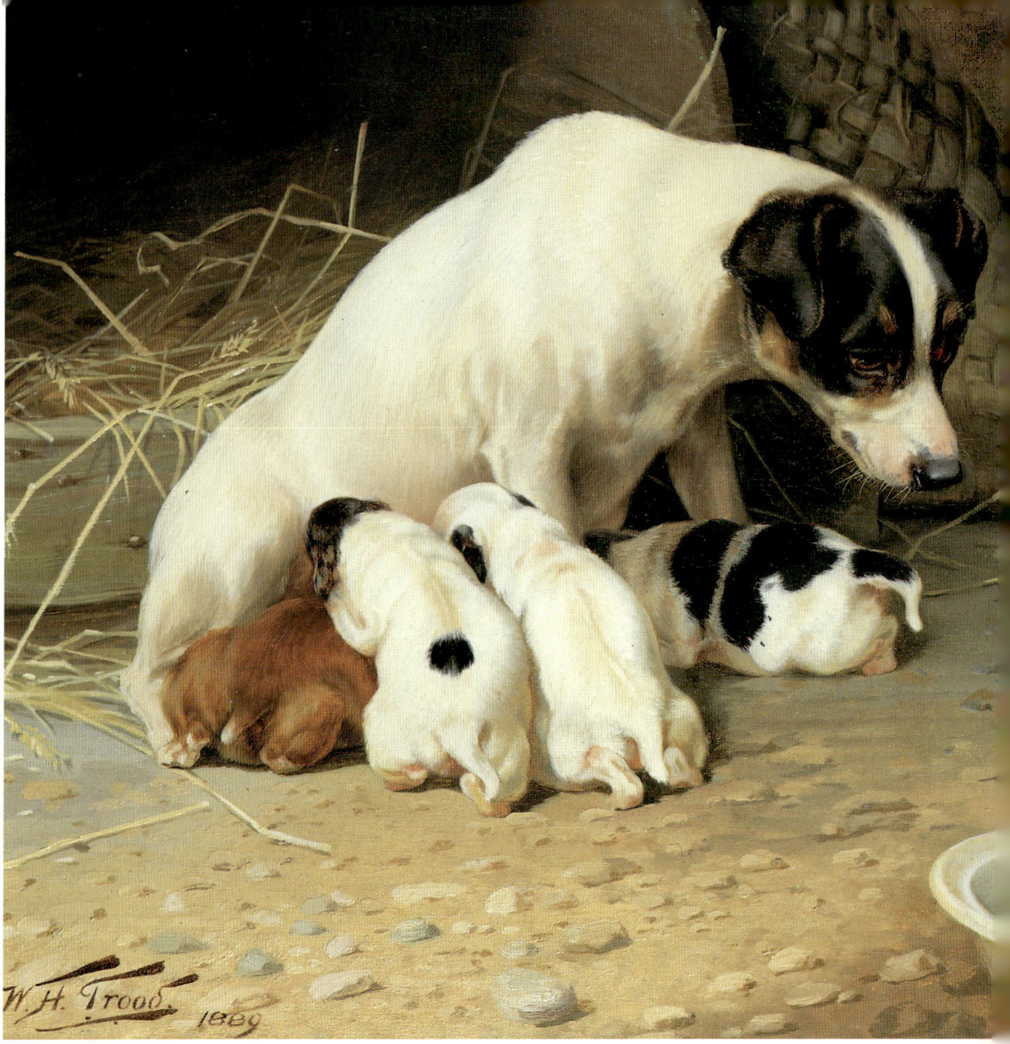

Smooth Fox Terrier and puppies, 1889, William Henry Hamilton Trood.

NAME ....

....

ADDRESS ....

....

....

....

TEL ....

....

FAX ....

NAME ....

....

ADDRESS ....

....

....

....

TEL ....

....

FAX ....

Buy a pup and your money will buy love unflinching that cannot lie. Rudyard Kipling

P

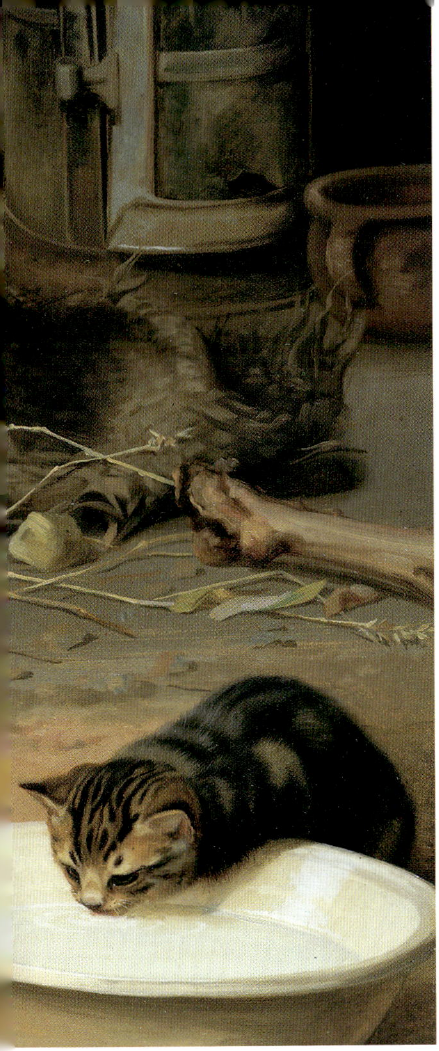

NAME

ADDRESS

TEL

FAX

NAME

ADDRESS

TEL

FAX

NAME

ADDRESS

TEL

FAX

NAME

ADDRESS

TEL

FAX

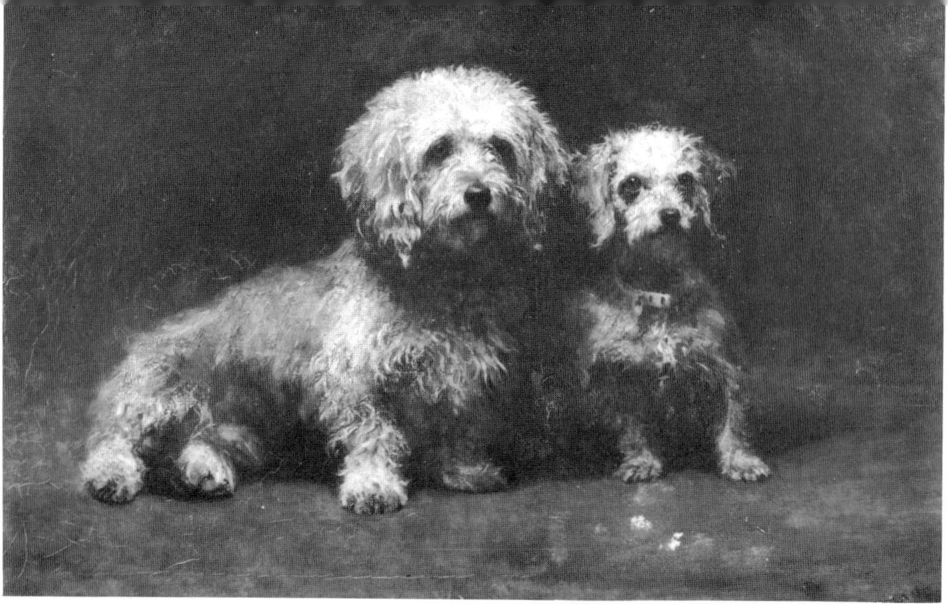

Dandie Dinmont and puppy, 1891, Helen Cridland.

NAME

ADDRESS

TEL

FAX

NAME

ADDRESS

TEL

FAX

NAME

ADDRESS

TEL

FAX

NAME

ADDRESS

TEL

FAX

Q

NAME

ADDRESS

TEL

FAX

NAME

ADDRESS

TEL

FAX

NAME

ADDRESS

TEL

FAX

NAME

ADDRESS

TEL

FAX

NAME

ADDRESS

TEL

FAX

NAME

ADDRESS

TEL

FAX

Q

'I've brought you a little dog . . . I had him brought down here in a large hamper labelled "Explosives", a title which appears to have been well selected.' G.K. Chesterton

NAME

ADDRESS

TEL

FAX

NAME

ADDRESS

TEL

FAX

NAME

ADDRESS

TEL

FAX

NAME

ADDRESS

TEL

FAX

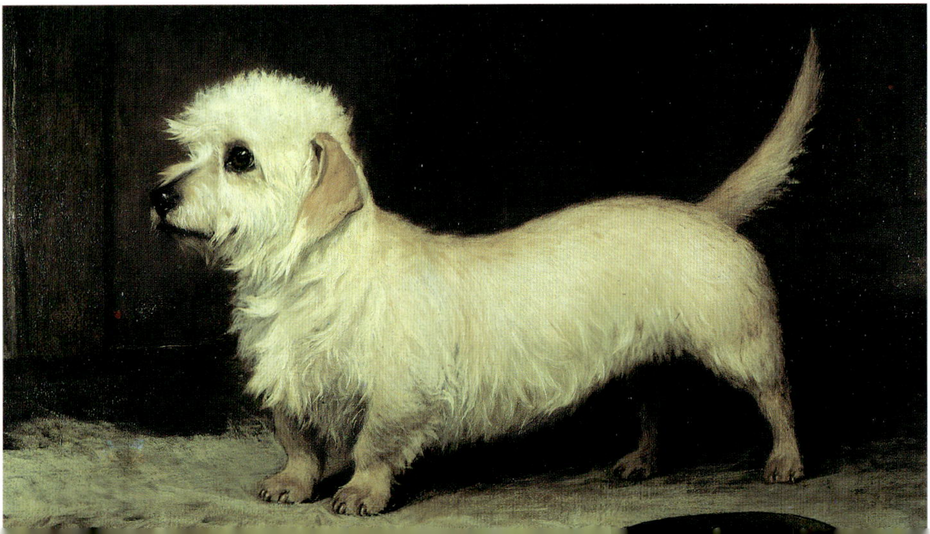

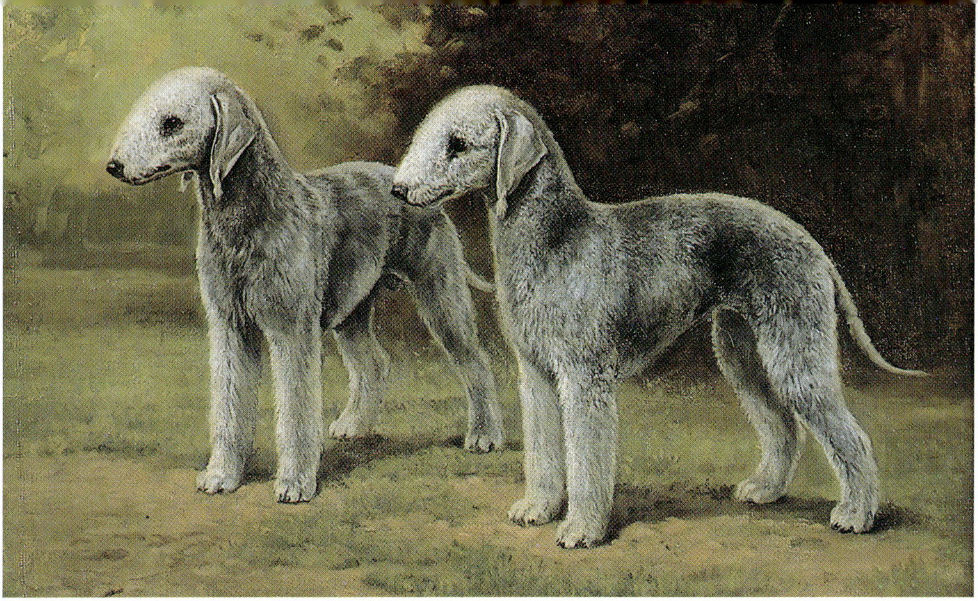

Bedlington Terriers, c.1941, Edwin Megargee.

NAME ....

....

ADDRESS ....

....

....

....

TEL ....

....

FAX ....

NAME ....

....

ADDRESS ....

....

....

....

TEL ....

....

FAX ....

NAME ....

....

ADDRESS ....

....

....

....

TEL ....

....

FAX ....

NAME ....

....

ADDRESS ....

....

....

....

TEL ....

....

FAX ....

Dandie Dinmont Terrier, 1899, Margaret Collyer.

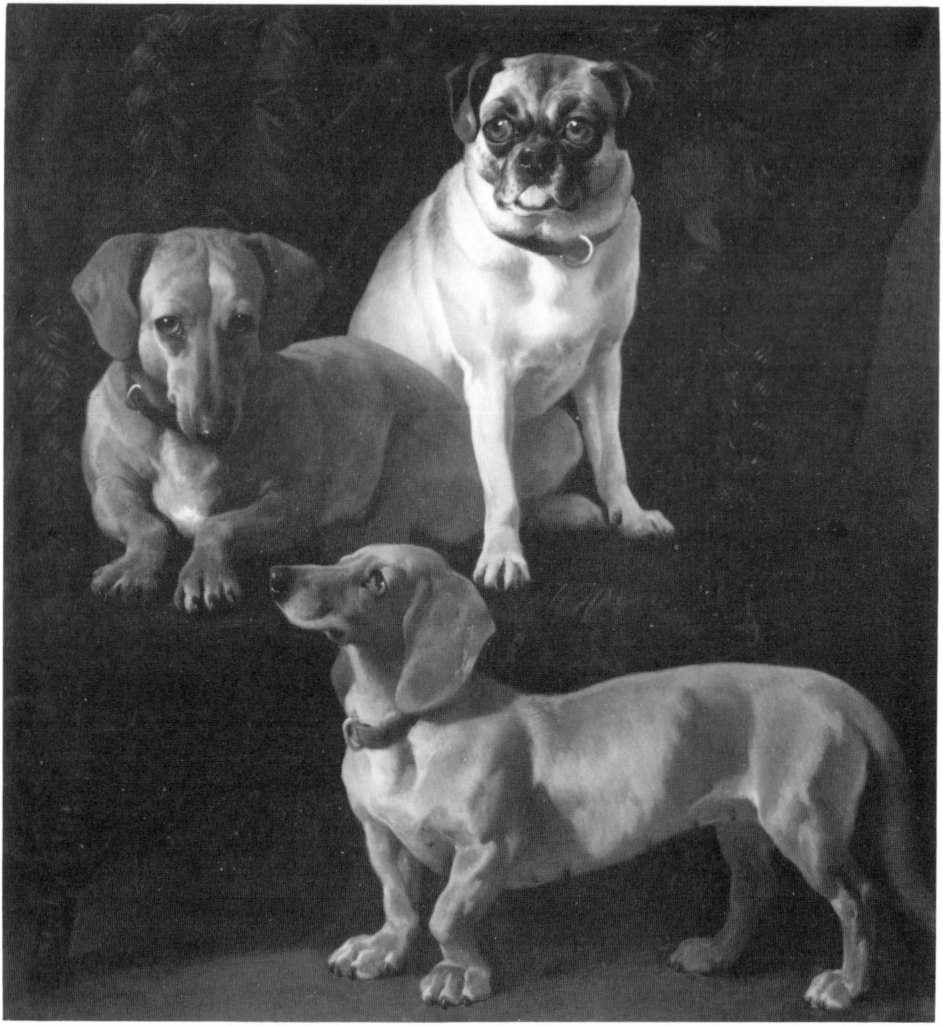

Dachshunds and Pug, c.1890, John Sargent Noble.

NAME ....

....

ADDRESS ....

....

....

....

TEL ....

....

FAX ....

NAME ....

....

ADDRESS ....

....

....

....

TEL ....

....

FAX ....

R

NAME

ADDRESS

TEL

FAX

NAME

ADDRESS

TEL

FAX

NAME

ADDRESS

TEL

FAX

NAME

ADDRESS

TEL

FAX

NAME

ADDRESS

TEL

FAX

NAME

ADDRESS

TEL

FAX

R

NAME

ADDRESS

TEL

FAX

NAME

ADDRESS

TEL

FAX

NAME

ADDRESS

TEL

FAX

NAME

ADDRESS

TEL

FAX

NAME

ADDRESS

TEL

FAX

NAME

ADDRESS

TEL

FAX

My dachshund . . . is the best and gentlest and most reasonable and well-mannered, as well as the most beautiful. Henry James

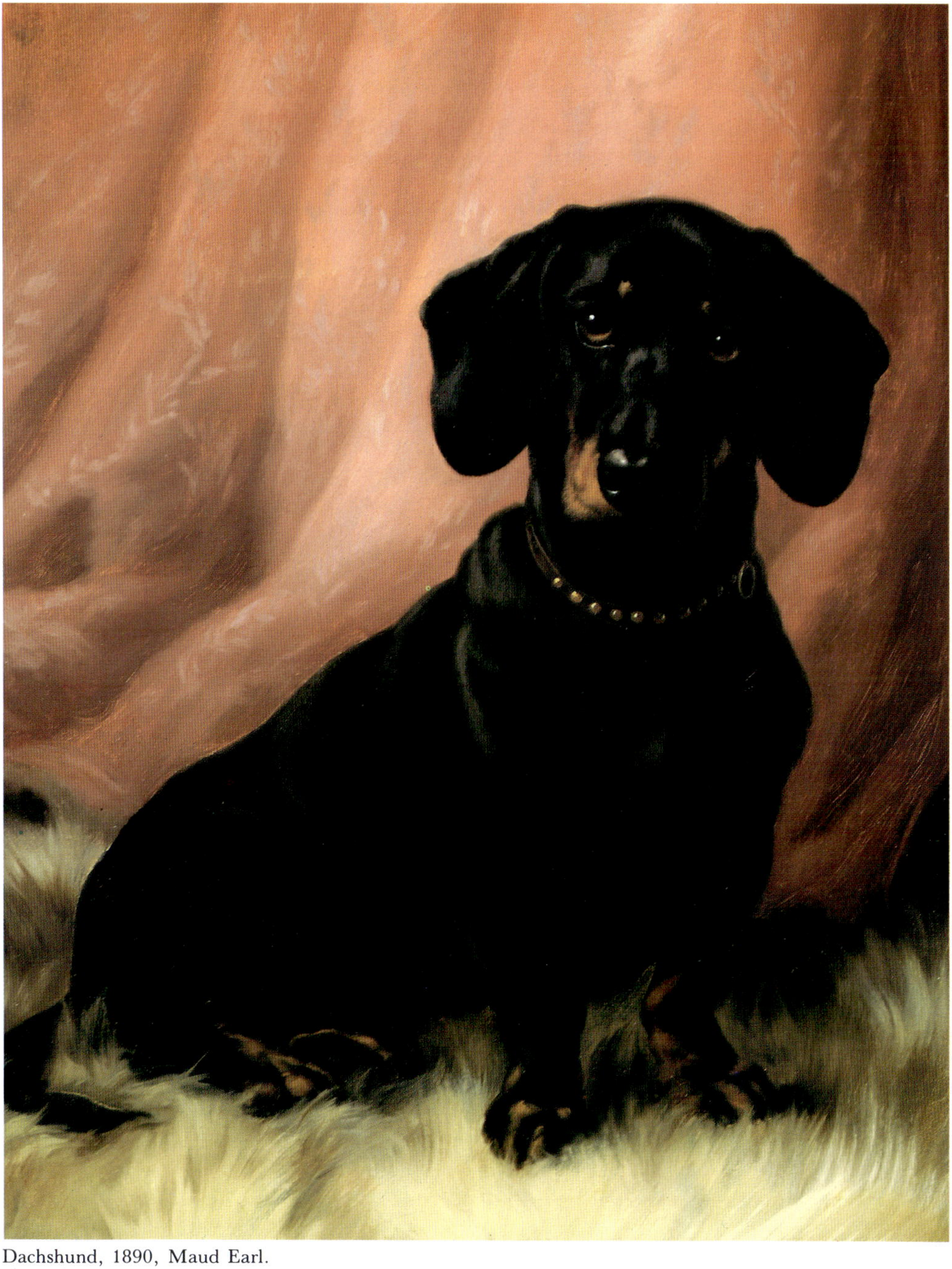

Dachshund, 1890, Maud Earl.

R

Until one has loved an animal, a part of one's soul remains unawakened. Anatole France

NAME

ADDRESS

TEL

FAX

NAME

ADDRESS

TEL

FAX

NAME

ADDRESS

TEL

FAX

NAME

ADDRESS

TEL

FAX

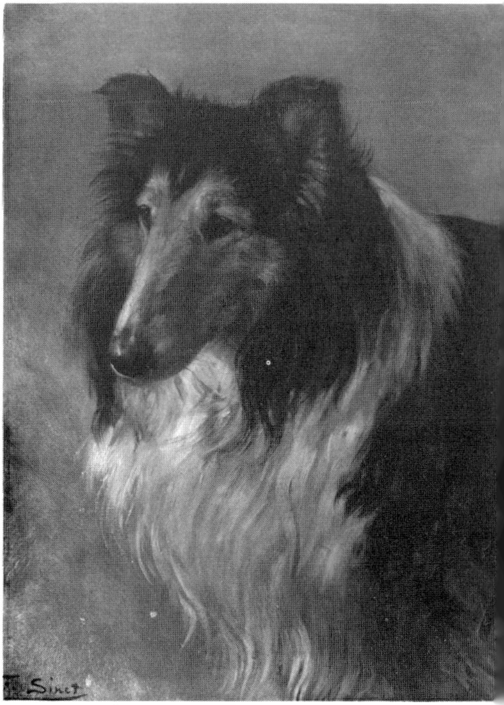

Collie, 1916, F. Sinet.

R

NAME

ADDRESS

TEL

FAX

NAME

ADDRESS

TEL

FAX

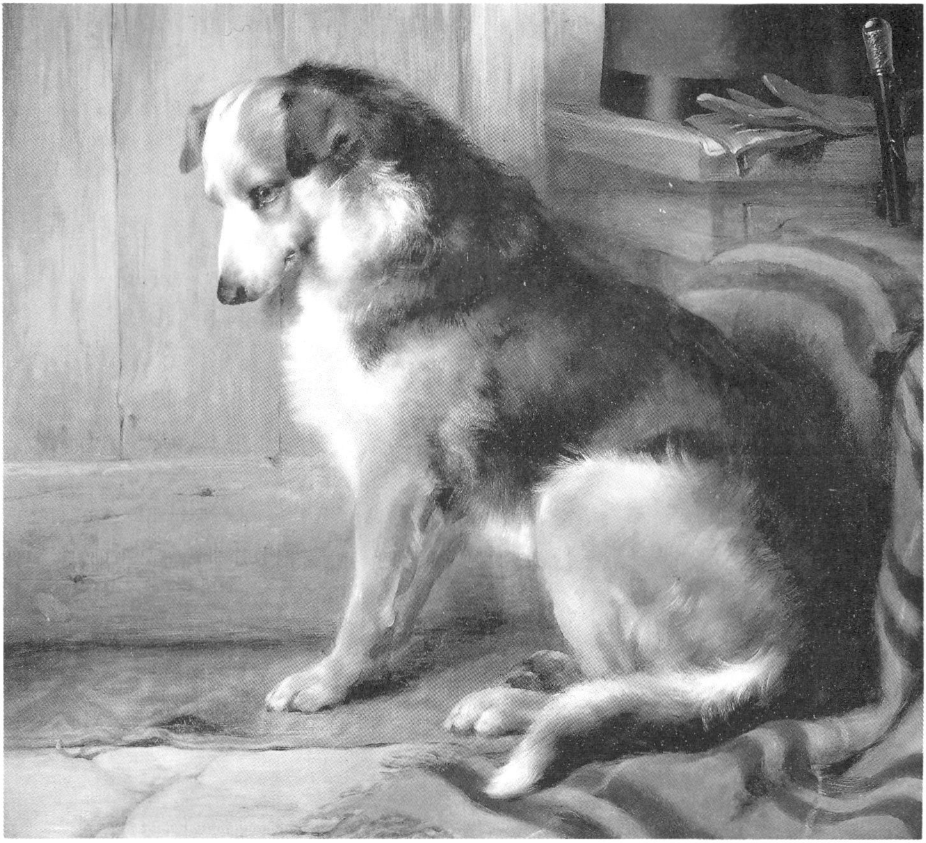

:ollie, c.1885, Edwin Douglas.

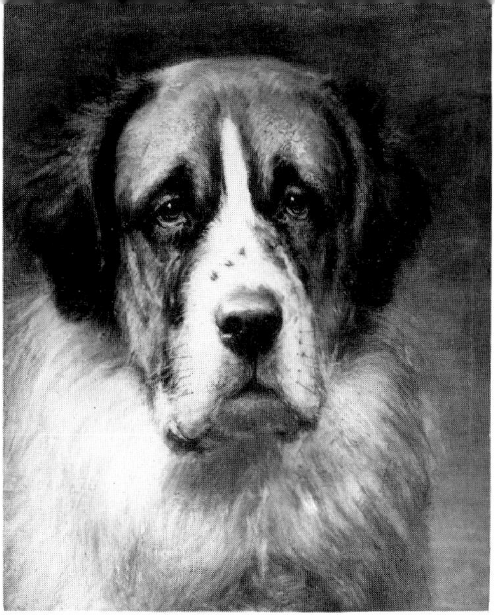

St. Bernard, c.1875, R.S. Moseley.

NAME ....

ADDRESS ....

TEL ....

FAX ....

NAME ....

ADDRESS ....

TEL ....

FAX ....

NAME ....

ADDRESS ....

TEL ....

FAX ....

NAME ....

ADDRESS ....

TEL ....

FAX ....

NAME ....

ADDRESS ....

TEL ....

FAX ....

S

NAME ....

....

ADDRESS ....

....

....

....

TEL ....

....

FAX ....

NAME ....

....

ADDRESS ....

....

....

....

TEL ....

....

FAX ....

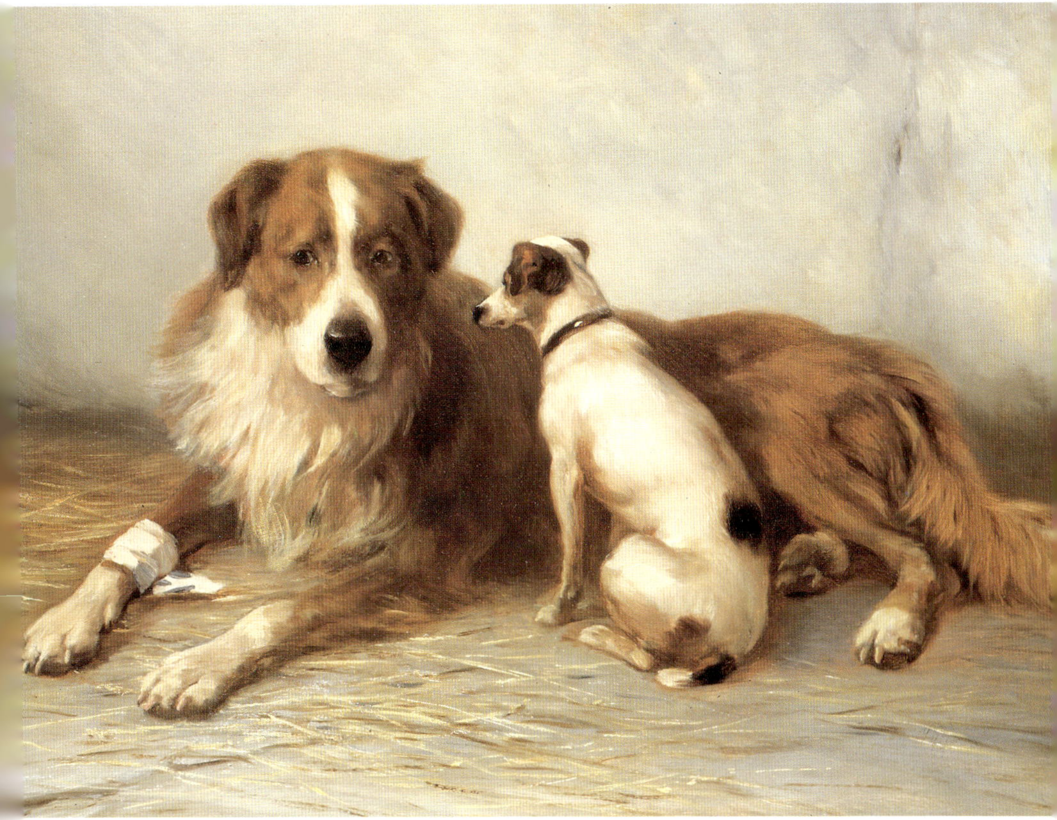

St. Bernard and Terrier, 1892, Henry Garland.

S

NAME

ADDRESS

TEL

FAX

NAME

ADDRESS

TEL

FAX

NAME

ADDRESS

TEL

FAX

NAME

ADDRESS

TEL

FAX

NAME

ADDRESS

TEL

FAX

NAME

ADDRESS

TEL

FAX

S

NAME
ADDRESS
TEL
FAX

NAME
ADDRESS
TEL
FAX

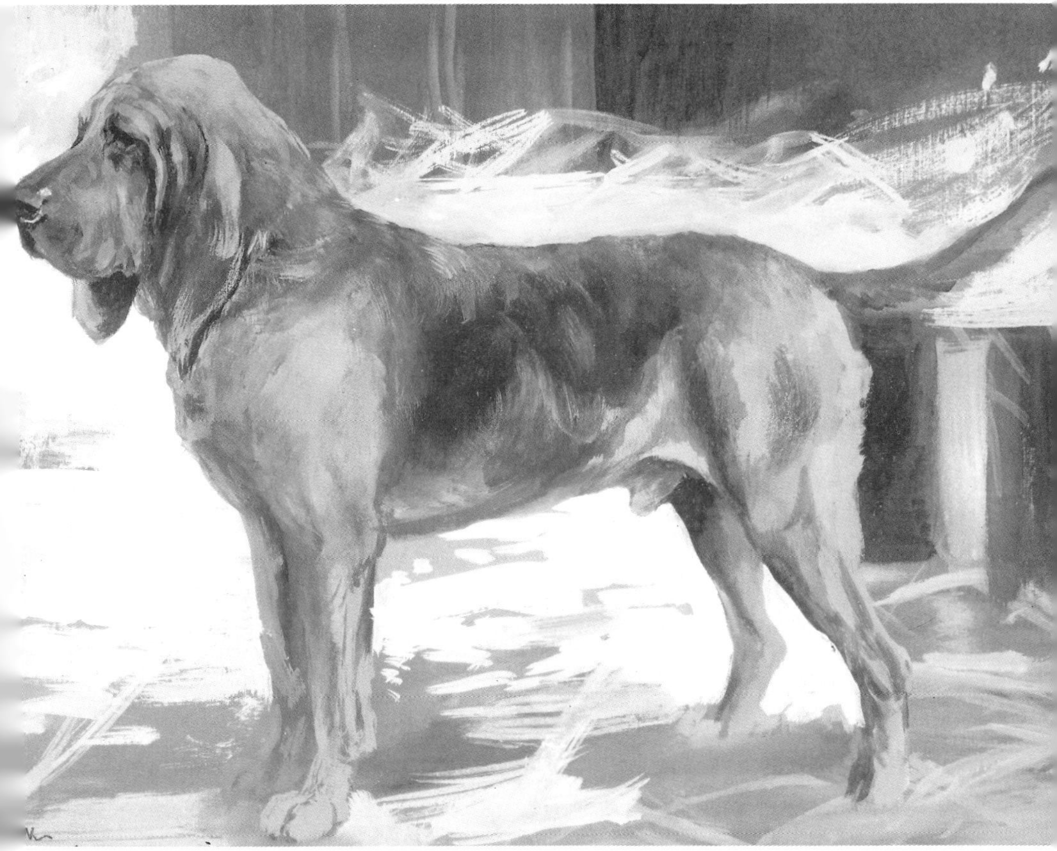

Bloodhound, 1935, Reuben Ward Binks.

S

NAME

ADDRESS

TEL

FAX

NAME

ADDRESS

TEL

FAX

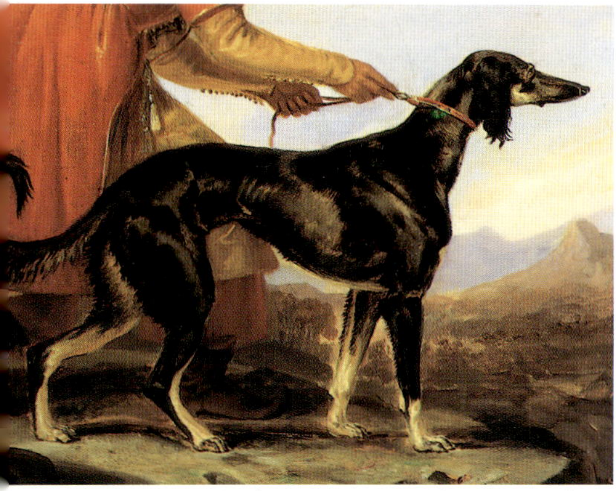

Saluki (Persian Greyhound), 1837, Charles Hamilton.

NAME

ADDRESS

TEL

FAX

NAME

ADDRESS

TEL

FAX

NAME

ADDRESS

TEL

FAX

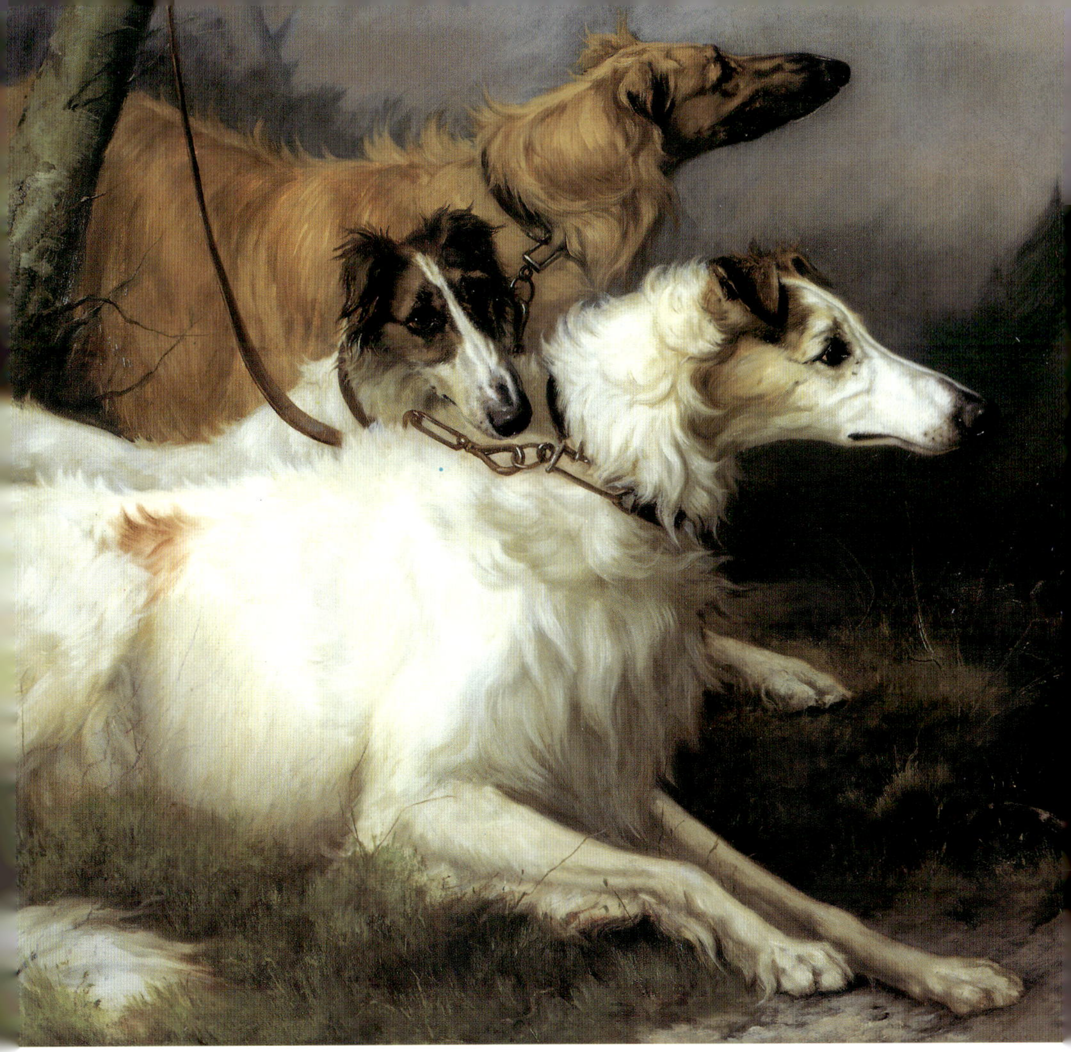

Borzois, 1892, Maud Earl.

NAME ....

....

ADDRESS ....

....

....

....

TEL ....

....

FAX ....

NAME ....

....

ADDRESS ....

....

....

....

TEL ....

....

FAX ....

S

NAME

ADDRESS

TEL

FAX

NAME

ADDRESS

TEL

FAX

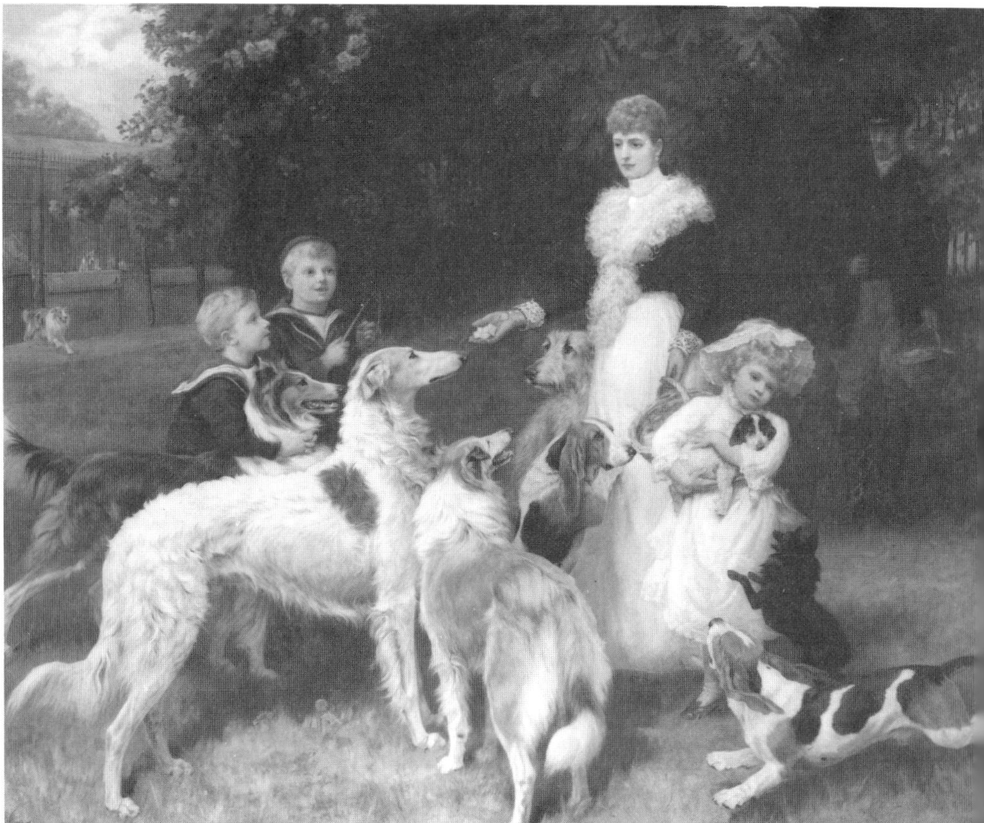

Queen Alexandra with her Grandchildren and Favourite Pets, 1902, Thomas Blinks and Fred Morgan.

S

The great pleasure of a dog is that you may make a fool of yourself with him and not only will he not scold you, but he will make a fool of himself too. Samuel Butler

NAME

ADDRESS

TEL

FAX

NAME

ADDRESS

TEL

FAX

NAME

ADDRESS

TEL

FAX

NAME

ADDRESS

TEL

FAX

NAME

ADDRESS

TEL

FAX

NAME

ADDRESS

TEL

FAX

T

NAME ....

....

ADDRESS ....

....

....

....

TEL ....

....

FAX ....

NAME ....

....

ADDRESS ....

....

....

....

TEL ....

....

FAX ....

NAME ....

....

ADDRESS ....

....

....

....

TEL ....

....

FAX ....

NAME ....

....

ADDRESS ....

....

....

....

TEL ....

....

FAX ....

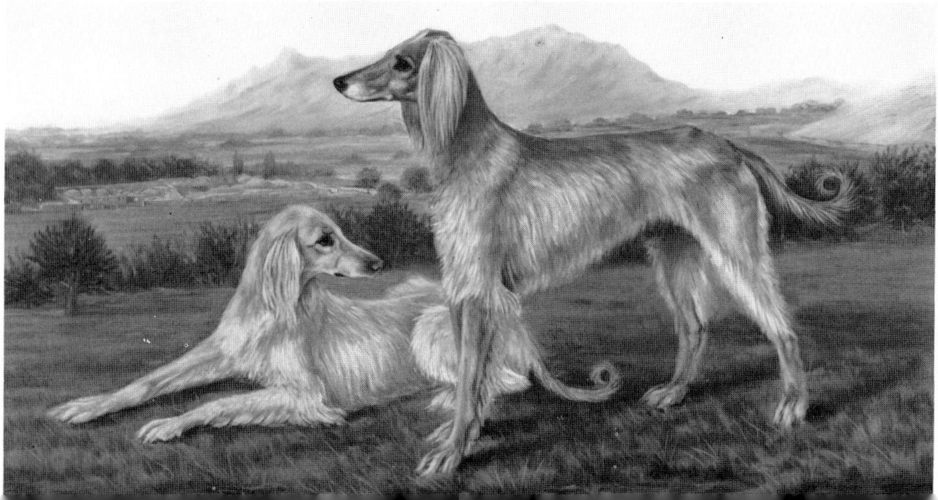

T

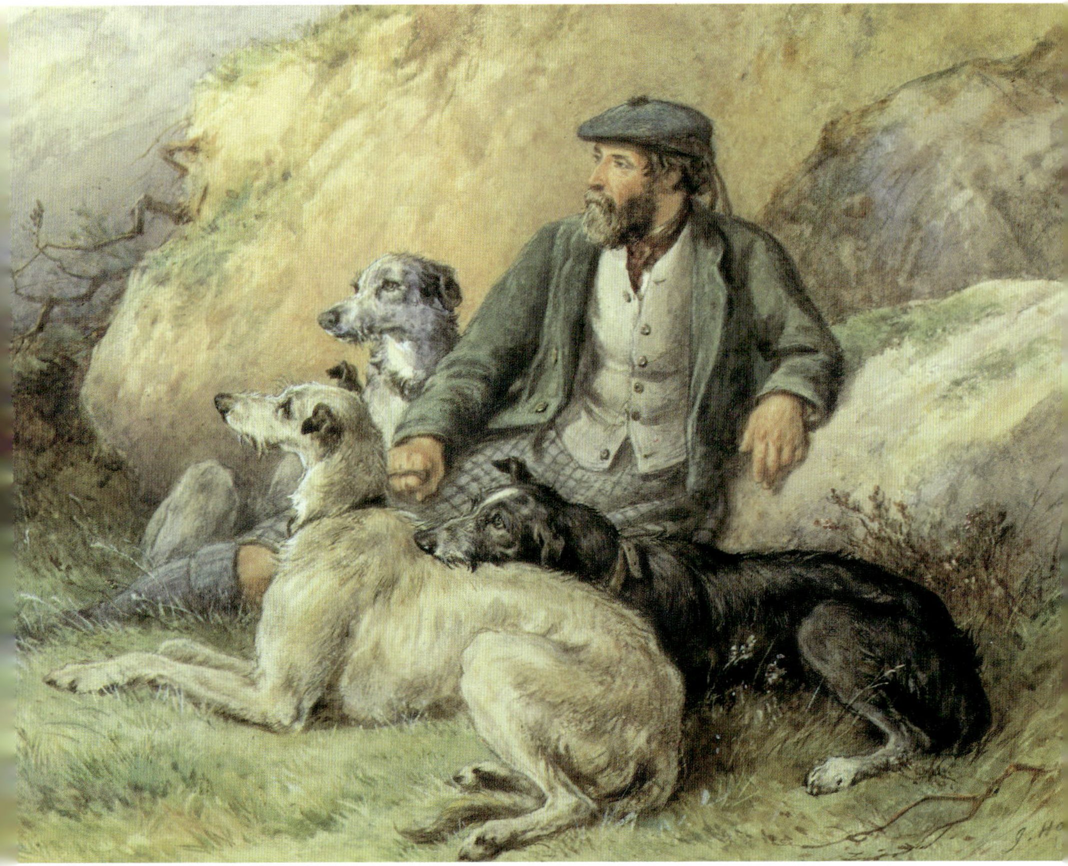

Deerhounds, 1872, James Hardy, Jnr.

NAME ....

....

ADDRESS ....

....

....

....

TEL ....

....

FAX ....

NAME ....

....

ADDRESS ....

....

....

....

TEL ....

....

FAX ....

Afghan Hounds, 1886, B.A. Hyland.

T

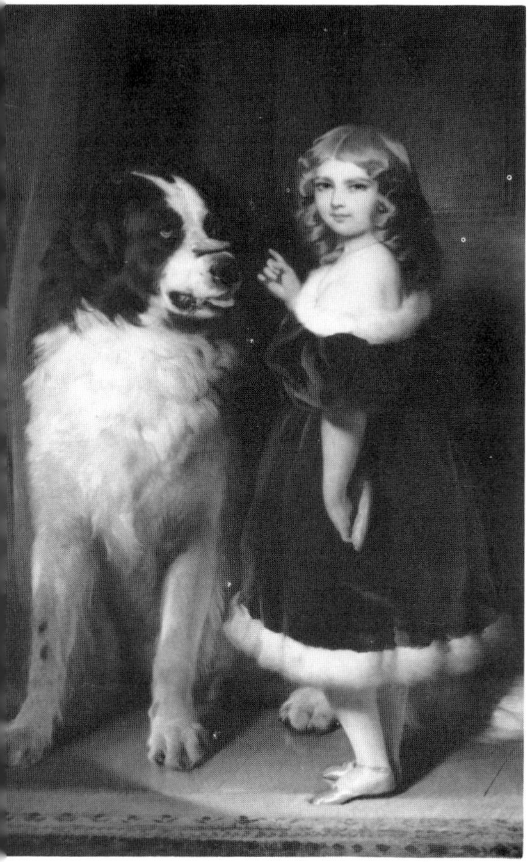

Newfoundland, c.1839, Edwin Landseer.

NAME ....

ADDRESS ....

TEL ....

FAX ....

NAME ....

ADDRESS ....

TEL ....

FAX ....

NAME ....

ADDRESS ....

TEL ....

FAX ....

NAME ....

ADDRESS ....

TEL ....

FAX ....

T

NAME

ADDRESS

TEL

FAX

NAME

ADDRESS

TEL

FAX

NAME

ADDRESS

TEL

FAX

NAME

ADDRESS

TEL

FAX

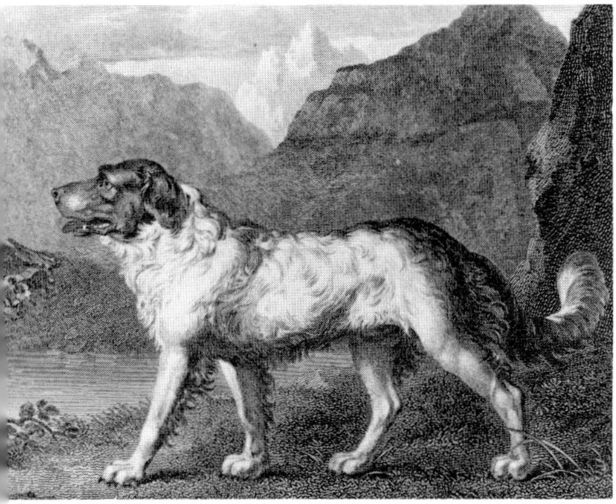

Newfoundland, 1803, Philip Reinagle.

NAME

ADDRESS

TEL

FAX

T

NAME ....

....

ADDRESS ....

....

....

....

TEL ....

....

FAX ....

NAME ....

....

ADDRESS ....

....

....

....

TEL ....

....

FAX ....

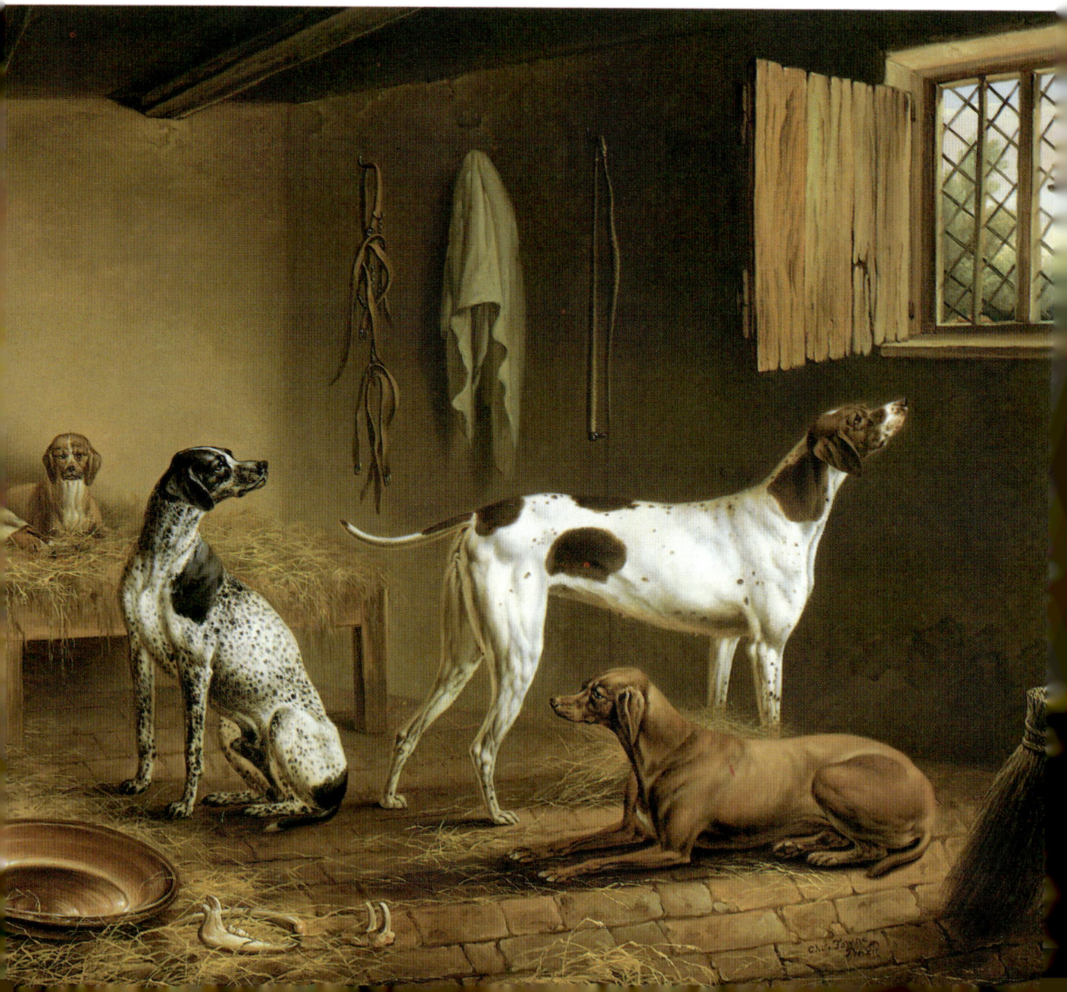

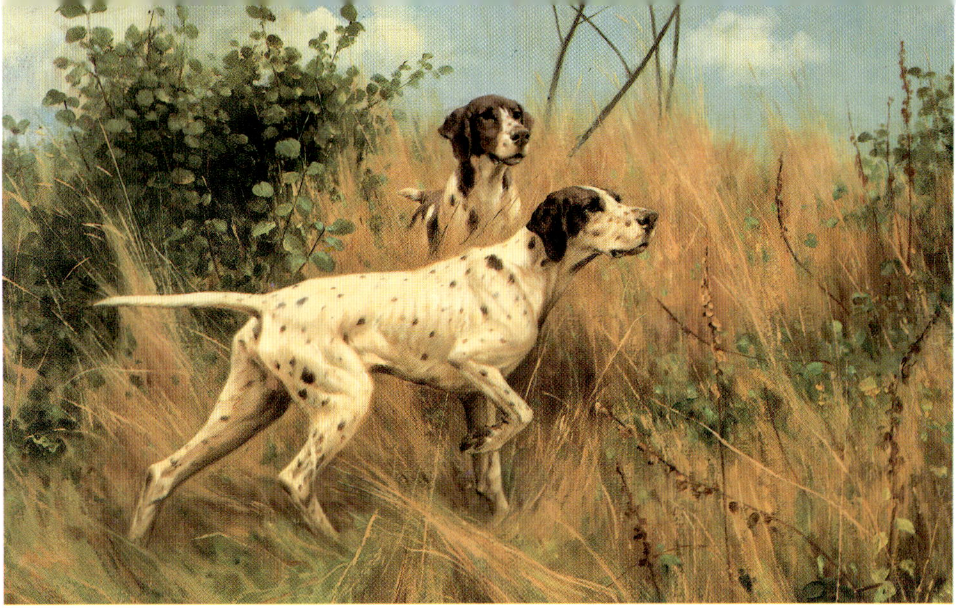

Pointers, Thomas Blinks.

NAME ....

....

ADDRESS ....

....

....

....

TEL ....

....

FAX ....

NAME ....

....

ADDRESS ....

....

....

....

TEL ....

....

FAX ....

NAME ....

....

ADDRESS ....

....

....

....

TEL ....

....

FAX ....

NAME ....

....

ADDRESS ....

....

....

....

TEL ....

....

FAX ....

Pointers, Charles Towne.

U

NAME

ADDRESS

TEL

FAX

NAME

ADDRESS

TEL

FAX

NAME

ADDRESS

TEL

FAX

NAME

ADDRESS

TEL

FAX

NAME

ADDRESS

TEL

FAX

NAME

ADDRESS

TEL

FAX

U

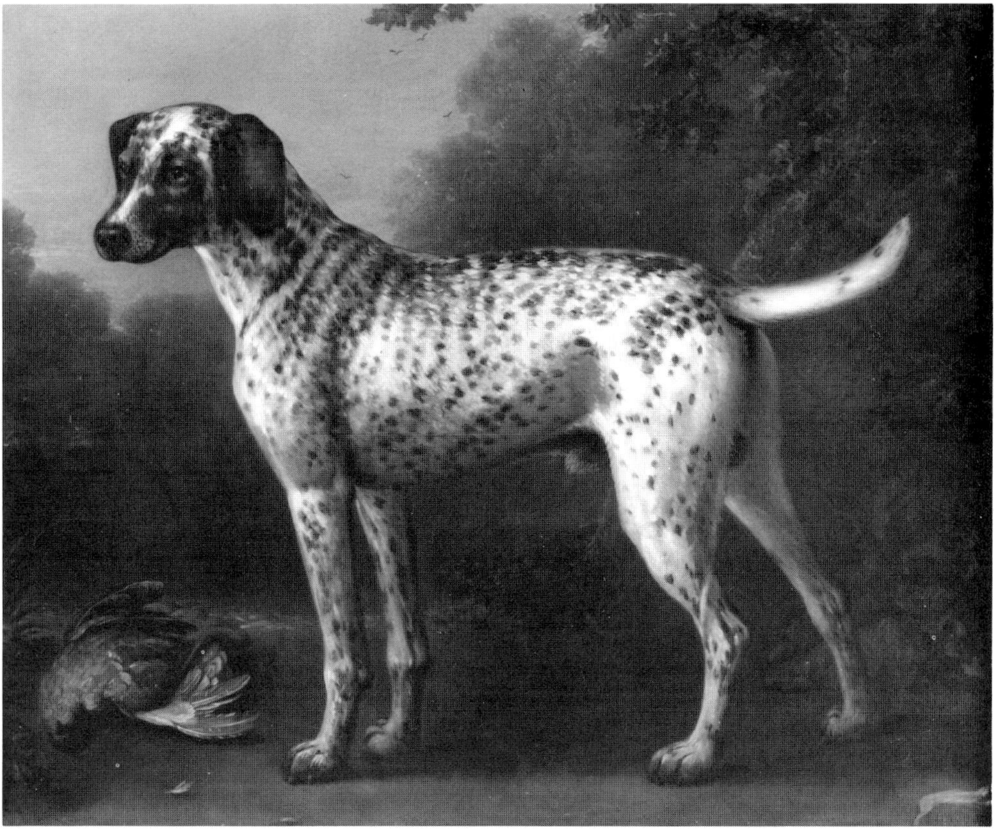

Spotted Pointer, 1738, John Wootton.

NAME ....

....

ADDRESS ....

....

....

....

TEL ....

....

FAX ....

NAME ....

....

ADDRESS ....

....

....

....

TEL ....

....

FAX ....

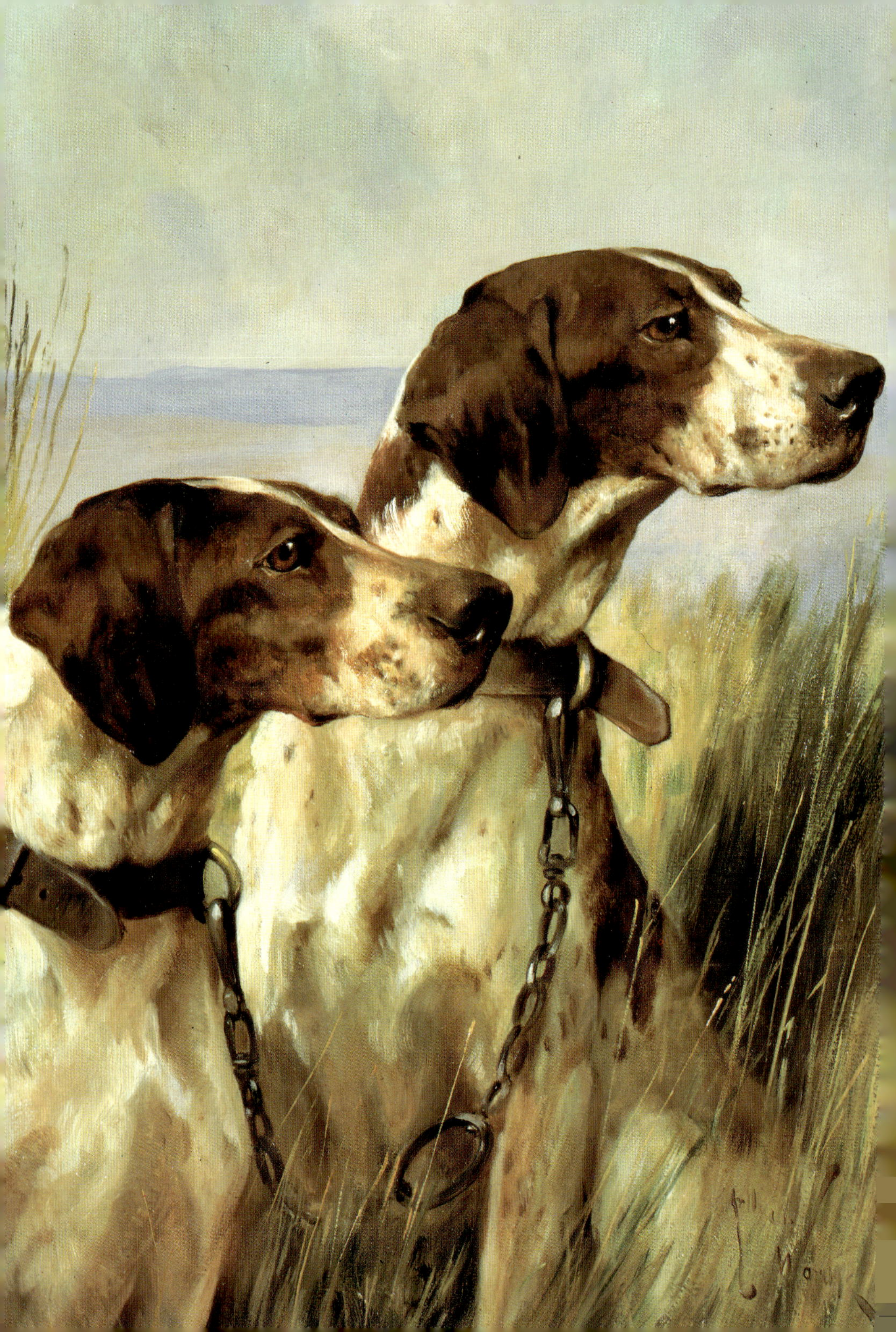

'Ah you should keep dogs – fine animals – sagacious creatures – dog of my own once – pointer – surprising instinct.'
Charles Dickens

U

NAME ....

ADDRESS ....

TEL ....

FAX ....

NAME ....

ADDRESS ....

TEL ....

FAX ....

NAME ....

ADDRESS ....

TEL ....

FAX ....

NAME ....

ADDRESS ....

TEL ....

FAX ....

NAME ....

ADDRESS ....

TEL ....

FAX ....

NAME ....

ADDRESS ....

TEL ....

FAX ....

Pointers, Arthur Wardle.

V

NAME

ADDRESS

TEL

FAX

NAME

ADDRESS

TEL

FAX

NAME

ADDRESS

TEL

FAX

NAME

ADDRESS

TEL

FAX

NAME

ADDRESS

TEL

FAX

NAME

ADDRESS

TEL

FAX

V

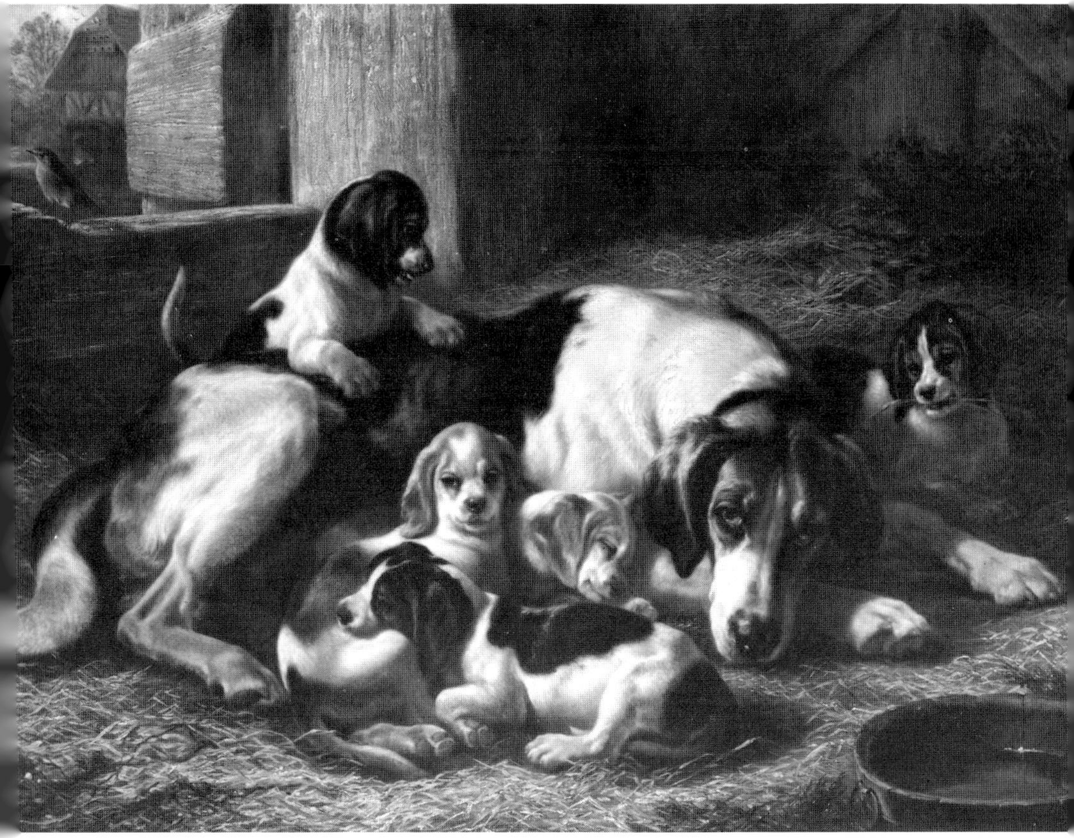

Foxhound and puppies, 1866, Samuel John Carter.

NAME ....

....

ADDRESS ....

....

....

....

TEL ....

....

FAX ....

NAME ....

....

ADDRESS ....

....

....

....

TEL ....

....

FAX ....

V

NAME

ADDRESS

TEL

FAX

NAME

ADDRESS

TEL

FAX

NAME

ADDRESS

TEL

FAX

NAME

ADDRESS

TEL

FAX

NAME

ADDRESS

TEL

FAX

NAME

ADDRESS

TEL

FAX

Foxhounds, Thomas Blinks.

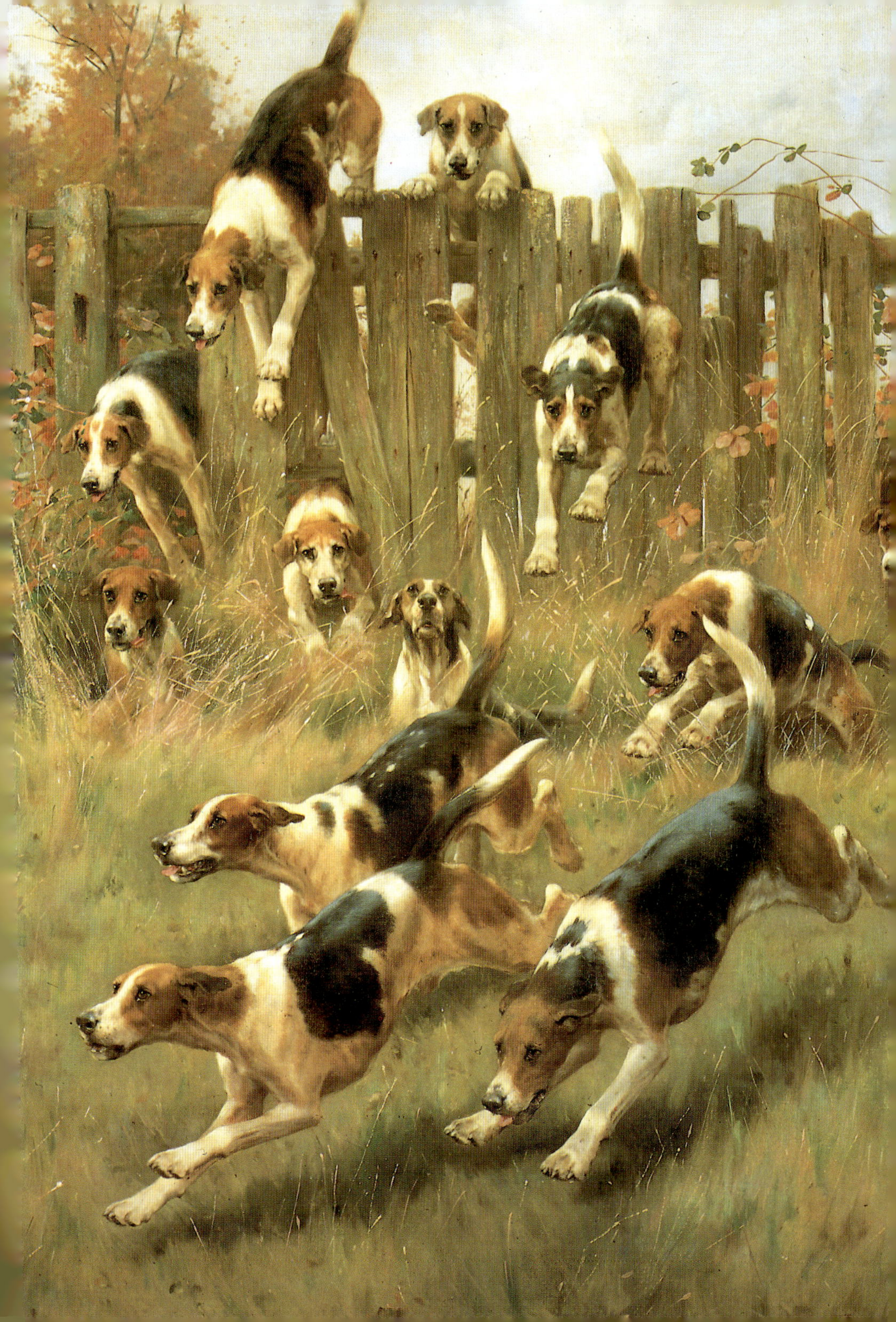

W

Dogs wave tails or plumes, according to breed, in several indicative ways. There is the wide sweep of expectancy, or the more vigorous movement of greeting. Or, tail under tummy, a subterranean waggle which can be pleasure tinged with guilt or fear. Elma Williams

NAME ....

ADDRESS ....

TEL ....

FAX ....

NAME ....

ADDRESS ....

TEL ....

FAX ....

NAME ....

ADDRESS ....

TEL ....

FAX ....

NAME ....

ADDRESS ....

TEL ....

FAX ....

NAME ....

ADDRESS ....

TEL ....

FAX ....

NAME ....

ADDRESS ....

TEL ....

FAX ....

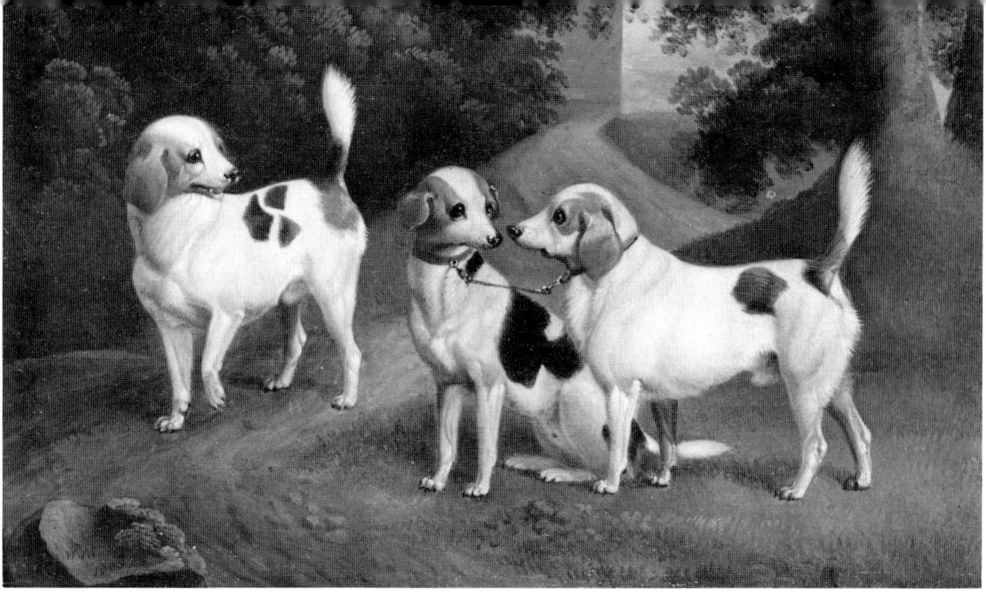

Beagles, 1808, W. Murray.

NAME ....

....

ADDRESS ....

....

....

....

TEL ....

....

FAX ....

NAME ....

....

ADDRESS ....

....

....

....

TEL ....

....

FAX ....

NAME ....

....

ADDRESS ....

....

....

....

TEL ....

....

FAX ....

NAME ....

....

ADDRESS ....

....

....

....

TEL ....

....

FAX ....

W

NAME ....

....

ADDRESS ....

....

....

....

TEL ....

....

FAX ....

NAME ....

....

ADDRESS ....

....

....

....

TEL ....

....

FAX ....

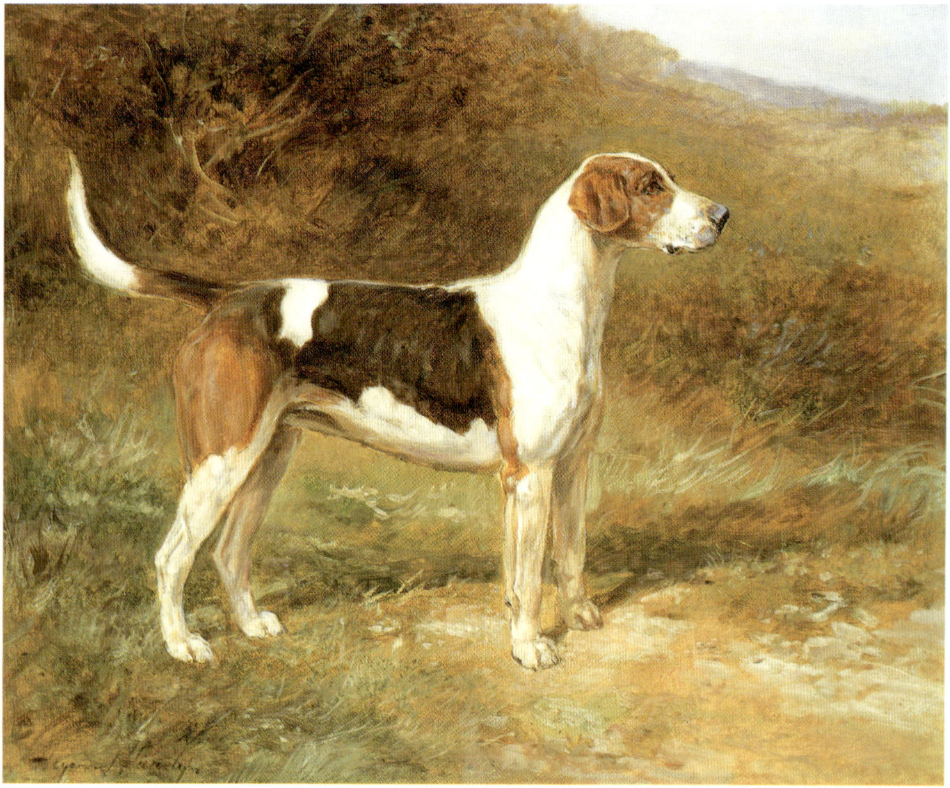

Foxhound, Heywood Hardy.

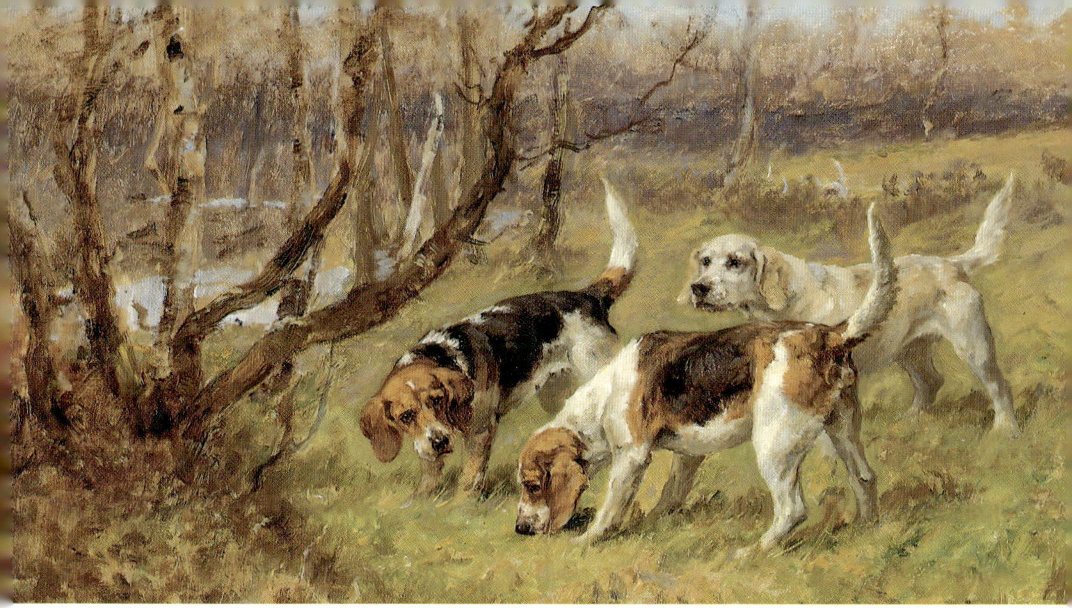

Beagles, c.1905, Maud Earl.

NAME ....

....

ADDRESS ....

....

....

....

TEL ....

....

FAX ....

NAME ....

....

ADDRESS ....

....

....

....

TEL ....

....

FAX ....

NAME ....

....

ADDRESS ....

....

....

....

TEL ....

....

FAX ....

NAME ....

....

ADDRESS ....

....

....

....

TEL ....

....

FAX ....

W

NAME

ADDRESS

TEL

FAX

NAME

ADDRESS

TEL

FAX

NAME

ADDRESS

TEL

FAX

NAME

ADDRESS

TEL

FAX

NAME

ADDRESS

TEL

FAX

NAME

ADDRESS

TEL

FAX

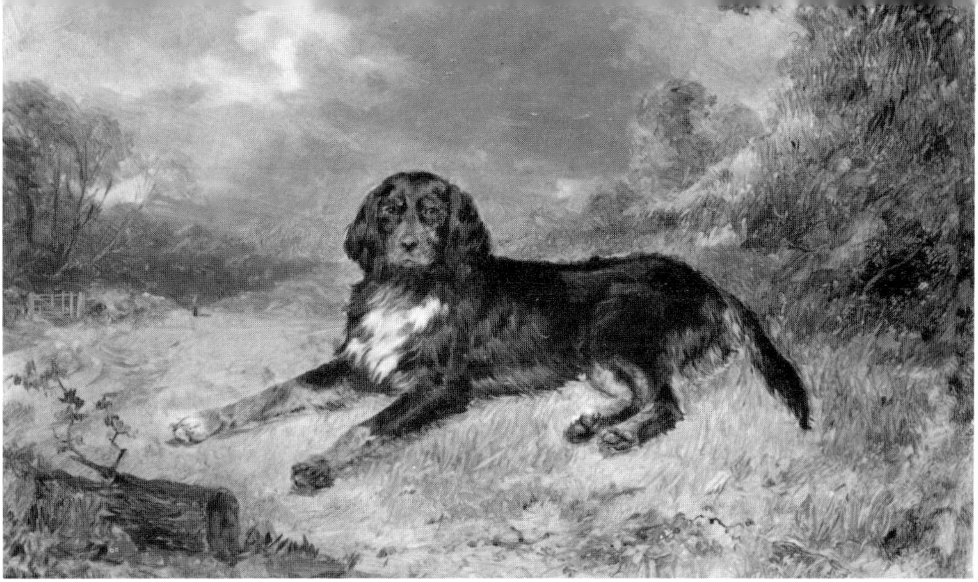

Gordon Setter, James Hardy, Jnr.

NAME ....

....

ADDRESS ....

....

....

....

TEL ....

....

FAX ....

NAME ....

....

ADDRESS ....

....

....

....

TEL ....

....

FAX ....

NAME ....

....

ADDRESS ....

....

....

....

TEL ....

....

FAX ....

NAME ....

....

ADDRESS ....

....

....

....

TEL ....

....

FAX ....

W

NAME

ADDRESS

TEL

FAX

NAME

ADDRESS

TEL

FAX

NAME

ADDRESS

TEL

FAX

NAME

ADDRESS

TEL

FAX

NAME

ADDRESS

TEL

FAX

NAME

ADDRESS

TEL

FAX

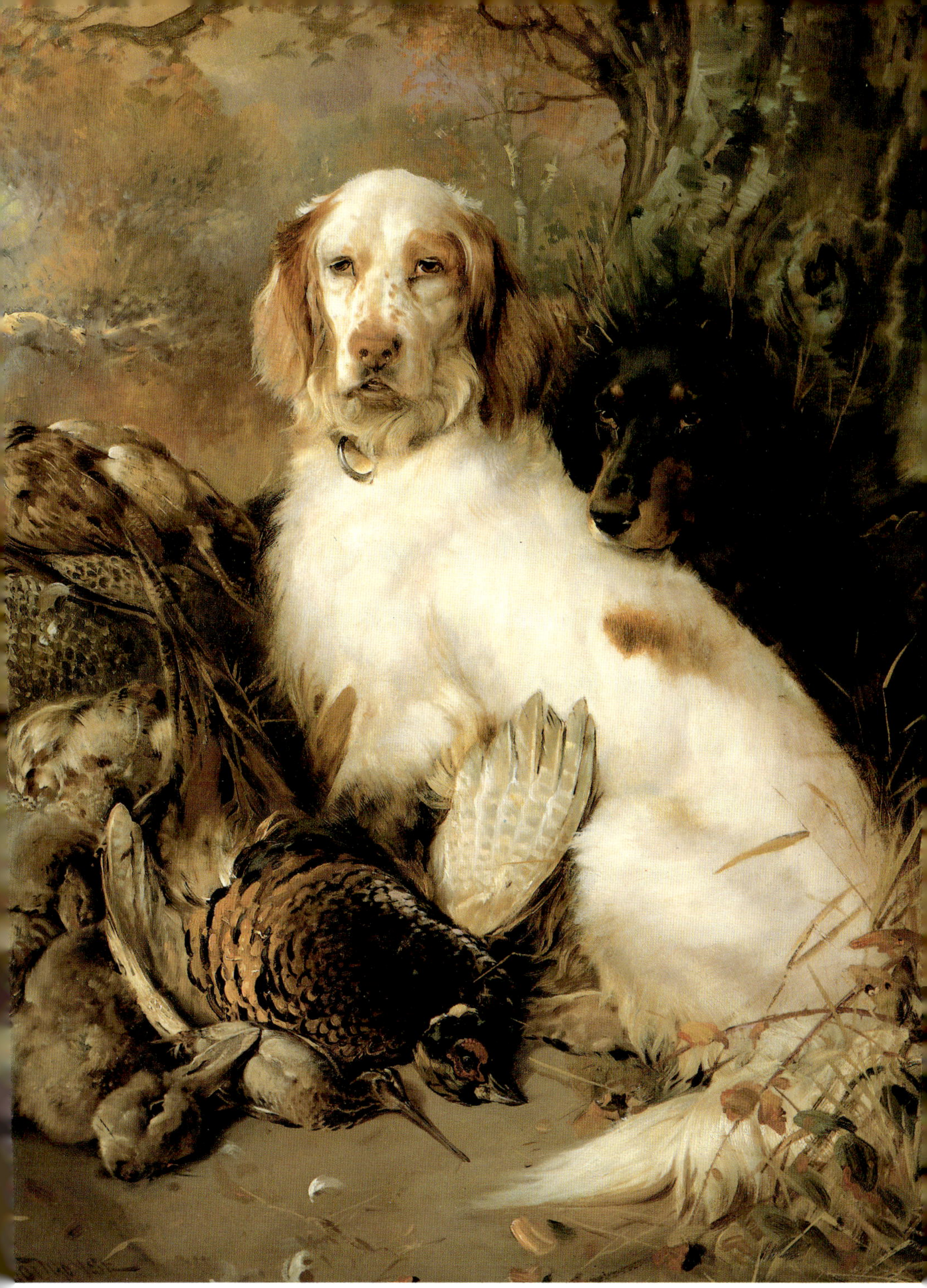

English and Gordon Setters, William Arnold Woodhouse.

X

NAME

ADDRESS

TEL

FAX

NAME

ADDRESS

TEL

FAX

NAME

ADDRESS

TEL

FAX

NAME

ADDRESS

TEL

FAX

NAME

ADDRESS

TEL

FAX

NAME

ADDRESS

TEL

FAX

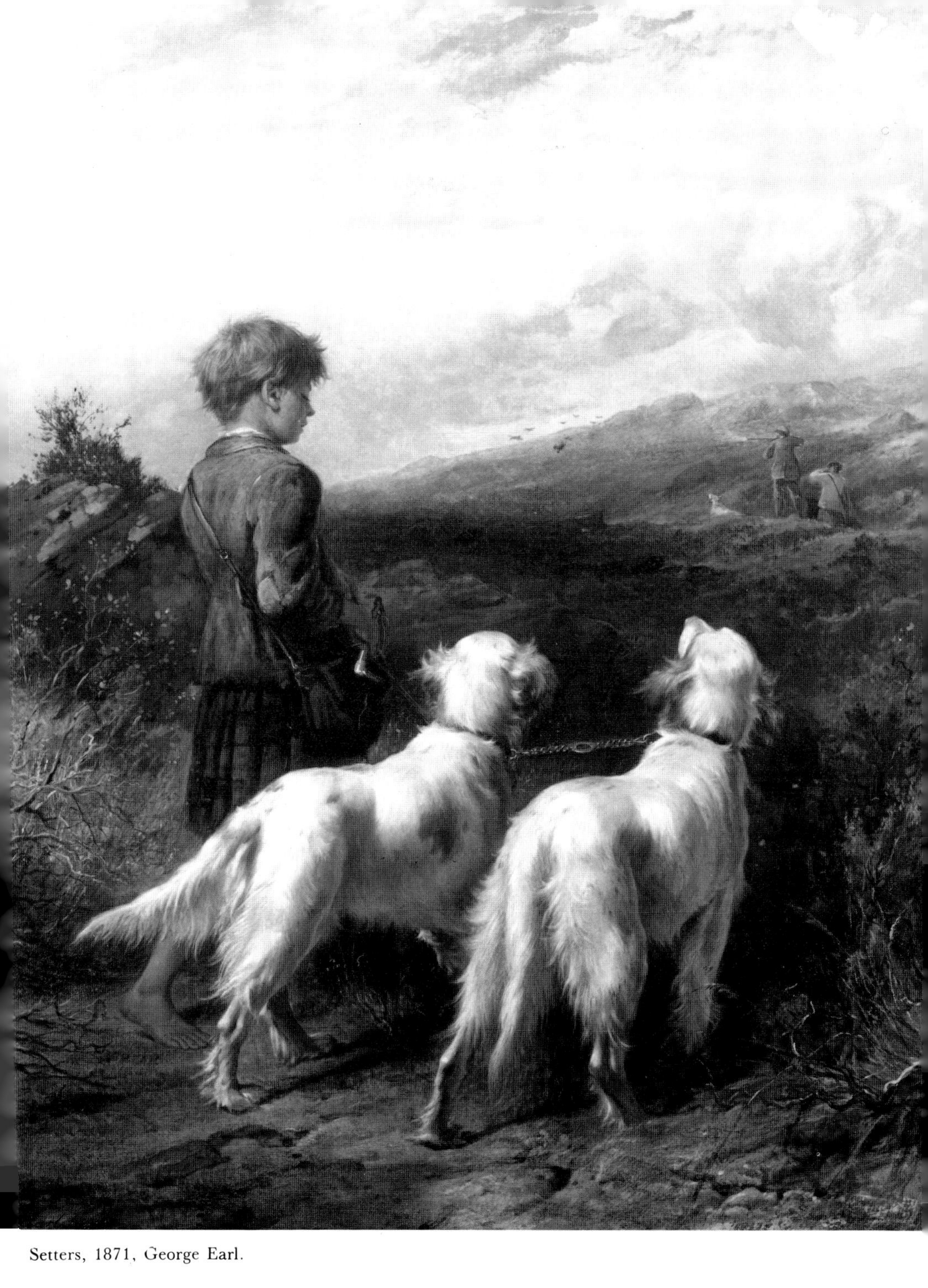

Setters, 1871, George Earl.

X

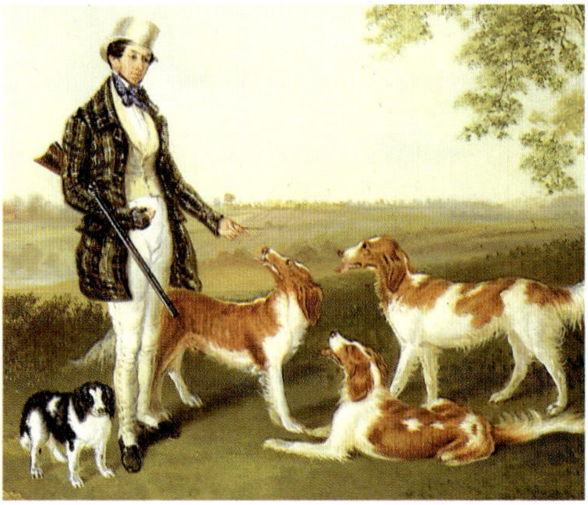

Spaniel and Setters, Thomas W. Bretland.

NAME ....

....

ADDRESS ....

....

....

....

TEL ....

....

FAX ....

NAME ....

....

ADDRESS ....

....

....

....

TEL ....

....

FAX ....

NAME ....

....

ADDRESS ....

....

....

....

TEL ....

....

FAX ....

NAME ....

....

ADDRESS ....

....

....

....

TEL ....

....

FAX ....

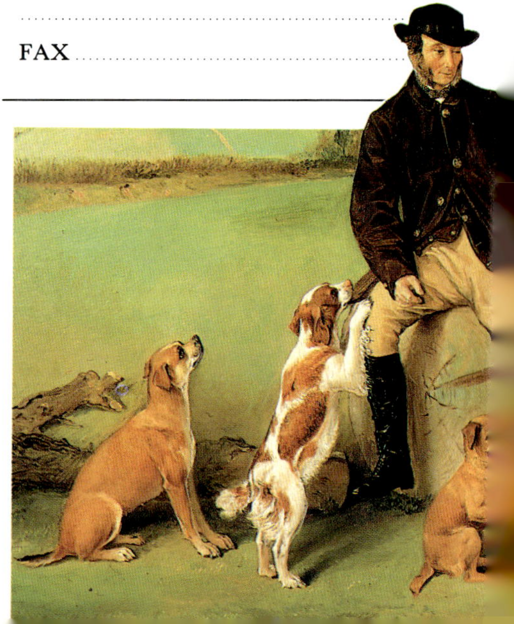

Spaniels and Irish Red and White Setters, E.F. Holt.

X

Man's most wonderful four-footed friend and companion, the dog. F.H. Bennett

NAME

ADDRESS

TEL

FAX

NAME

ADDRESS

TEL

FAX

NAME

ADDRESS

TEL

FAX

NAME

ADDRESS

TEL

FAX

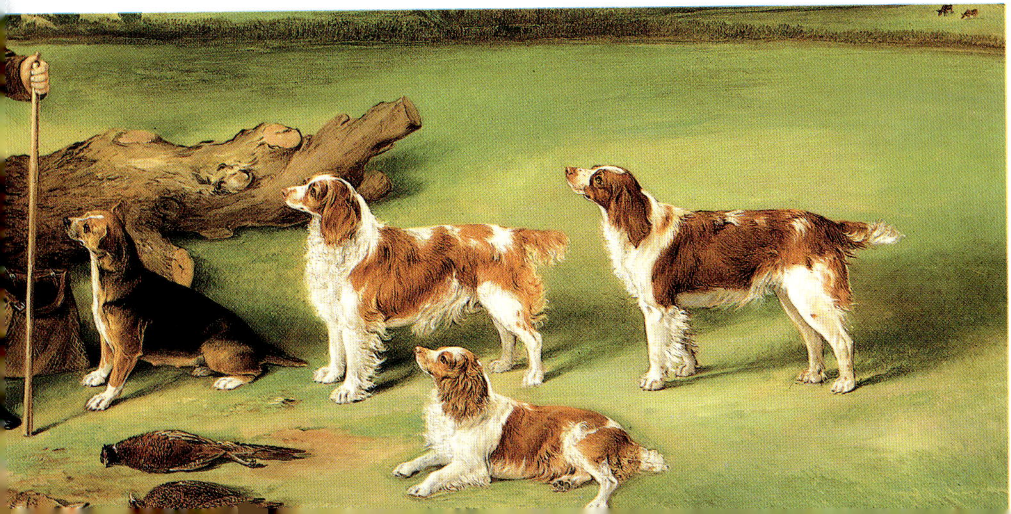

Y

NAME

ADDRESS

TEL

FAX

NAME

ADDRESS

TEL

FAX

NAME

ADDRESS

TEL

FAX

NAME

ADDRESS

TEL

FAX

NAME

ADDRESS

TEL

FAX

NAME

ADDRESS

TEL

FAX

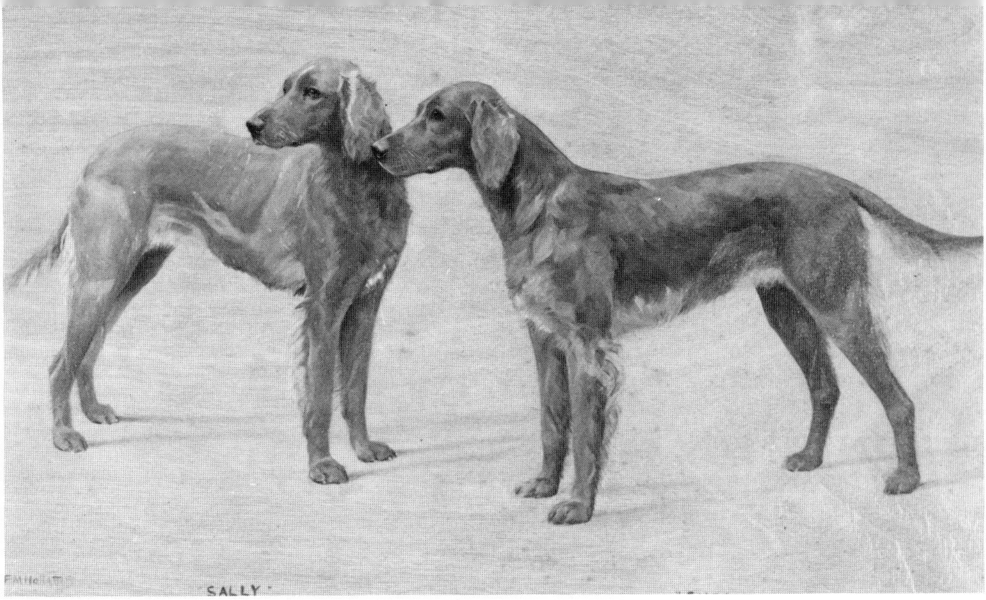

Irish Setters, F. Mabel Hollams.

NAME

ADDRESS

TEL

FAX

NAME

ADDRESS

TEL

FAX

NAME

ADDRESS

TEL

FAX

NAME

ADDRESS

TEL

FAX

Y

NAME

ADDRESS

TEL

FAX

NAME

ADDRESS

TEL

FAX

NAME

ADDRESS

TEL

FAX

NAME

ADDRESS

TEL

FAX

NAME

ADDRESS

TEL

FAX

NAME

ADDRESS

TEL

FAX

Irish, Gordon and English Setters, 1883, James Hardy, Jnr.

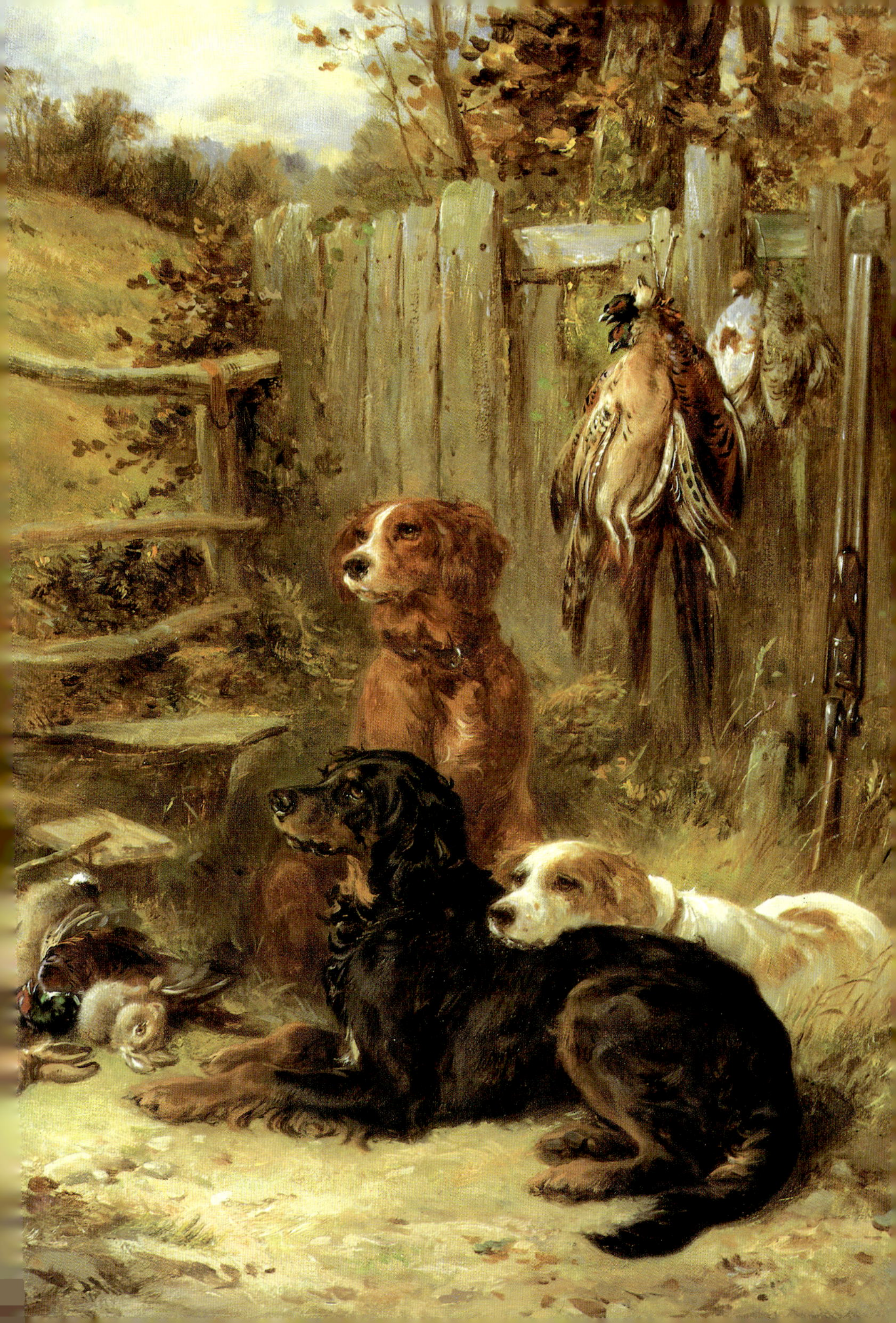

Z

NAME

ADDRESS

TEL

FAX

NAME

ADDRESS

TEL

FAX

NAME

ADDRESS

TEL

FAX

NAME

ADDRESS

TEL

FAX

NAME

ADDRESS

TEL

FAX

NAME

ADDRESS

TEL

FAX

Z

NAME

ADDRESS

TEL

FAX

NAME

ADDRESS

TEL

FAX

NAME

ADDRESS

TEL

FAX

NAME

ADDRESS

TEL

FAX

NAME

ADDRESS

TEL

FAX

NAME

ADDRESS

TEL

FAX